AF820471

ODWARD

MAP OF THE

Logging Railroads and Lumber Flumes of the Southern Sierra Nevada 1874 to 1942

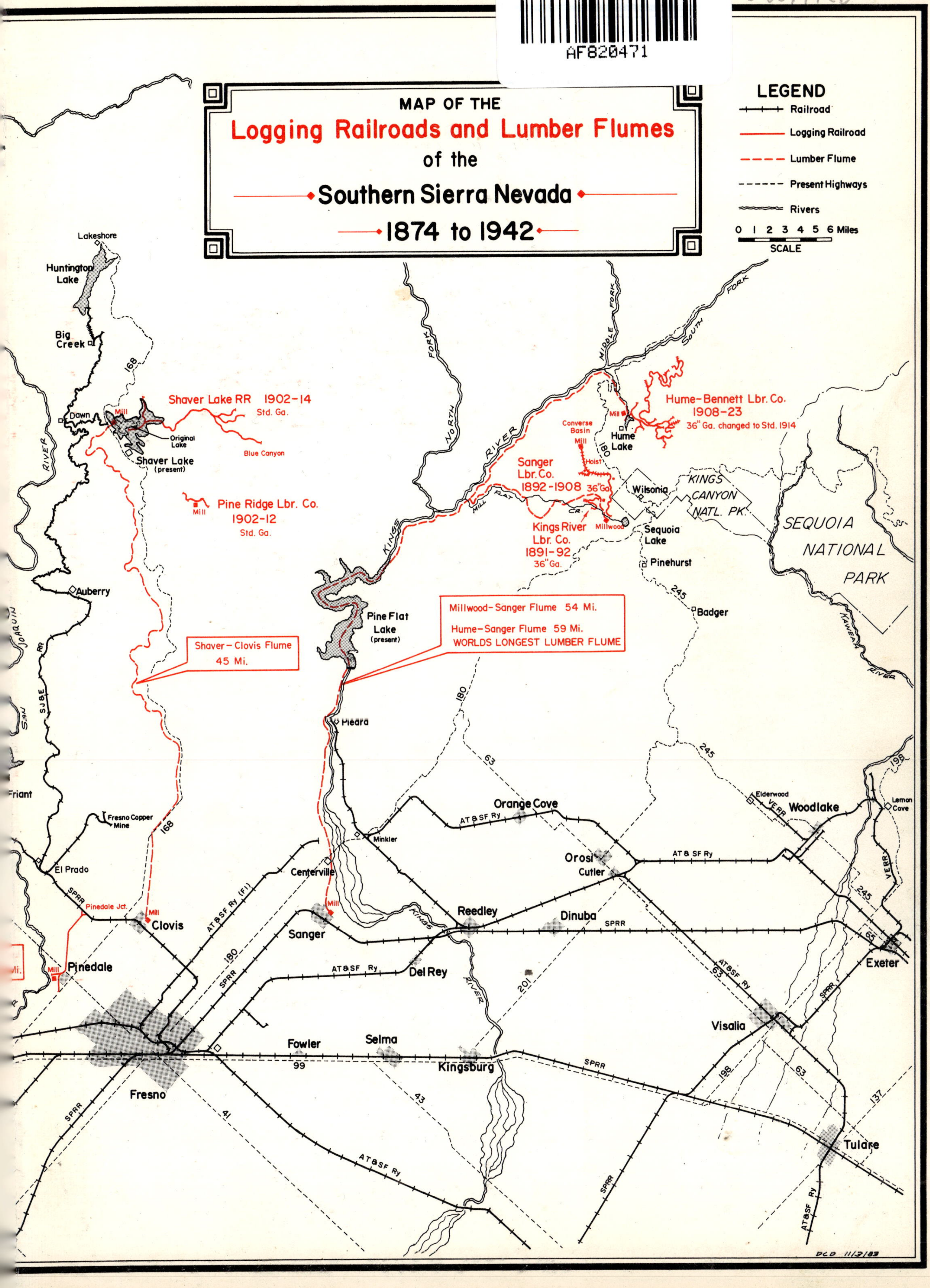

W. S. Woodward
11/84
Durham, N.H.

The Whistles Blow No More

Other books by Hank Johnston:

Rails to the Minarets
Railroads of the Yosemite Valley
Thunder in the Mountains
They Felled the Redwoods
Short Line to Paradise
The Railroad that Lighted Southern California
Death Valley Scotty: The Fastest Con in the West

Strong Man of the Sierra

The Shay locomotive was the principal reason the six railroad loggers were able to negotiate the steep terrain of the southern Sierra with their log trains during the Age of Steam. Madera Sugar Pine's No. 2, the *Arthur Hill,* posed for this photograph on a Fourth of July (note flag) early in the century just north of Fish Camp. The old road to Yosemite National Park, now Highway 41, may be seen just behind the locomotive. The headlight burned kerosene, and the plate below the link-and-pin coupling pocket in the front was used to push trains from the rear when double-heading.

The Whistles Blow No More

Railroad Logging in the Sierra Nevada 1874–1942

By Hank Johnston

Trans-Anglo Books
Glendale, California

Billy Woodward
Dunham

The Whistles Blow No More

Railroad Logging in the Sierra Nevada 1874-1942

© 1984 by Hank Johnston

All rights reserved. No part of this book may be reproduced or transmitted in any form or by any means, either electronic, mechanical, or other process, including photocopying, recording, or by any information storage and retrieval system, without permission in writing from the Publisher.

Library of Congress Cataloging in Publication Data

Johnston, Hank.
The whistles blow no more.

Includes index.
1. Logging railroads—Sierra Nevada Mountains (Calif. and Nev.)—History. I. Title.
TF25.S54J64 1984 385'.54'097944 83-18203
ISBN 0-87046-067-6

Printed and bound in the United States of America
Published by Trans-Anglo Books
P. O. Box 6444 Glendale, California 91205

Book Design by the Author
FIRST EDITION

Table of Contents

This large double-drum donkey was typical of the steam-powered yarding equipment used in moving logs during the chute-logging era. The scene is on the Sanger Lumber Company's Converse Basin operation circa 1905. (Harold Schutt Collection)

Introduction

THIS BOOK is a pictorial account of the glory days of flume and railroad logging in California's southern Sierra Nevada mountains. They lasted, intermittently, for just 68 seasons and involved only six operations, but they typified nearly everything that was exciting about steam logging out West.

Superlatives abound in the basic facts alone: There was the West's grandest sawmill, and its plushest lumber camp. There were the two steepest logging inclines, the three longest lumber flumes, and the fanciest logging railroad ever built. And—tragically—there was also the most destructive lumbering ever known, in which thousands of the biggest trees on earth were indiscriminately felled to no one's profit.

It all started in 1874, when the California Lumber Company began building its 52-mile V-flume from the mountains near present Oakhurst to Madera in the San Joaquin Valley. It ended in November 1942 when the last trainload of logs rolled to the mill pond of the Yosemite Sugar Pine Lumber Company at Merced Falls. In the intervening years, nearly five billion board feet of lumber were shipped down the slopes of the southern Sierra to markets all over the world. At final count, more than 500 miles of railroad track, 170 miles of lumber flumes, 28 locomotives, 16 sawmills, and thousands of boomer lumberjacks had been employed.

It all happened along a narrow mountainside strip between Sequoia and Yosemite National Parks, barely a hundred air miles long, but it left a legacy throughout central California in the form of five San Joaquin Valley towns, numerous Sierra lakes and resorts, and several hundred miles of old railroad grades now used as back-country automobile roads.

For the past 25 years, I've been collecting photographs and information about southern Sierra steam logging. Along the way, this has resulted in a half-dozen pictorial books (all published by Trans-Anglo Books) dealing in one form or another with the corporate histories of five of the six railroad loggers. It seemed to me, however, that one last book was needed to bring the picture into focus, as a sort of "summing up." What I wanted to do, basically, was provide an overview of the general southern Sierra logging scene of the time, one that would point out the different methods employed in getting timber out of the mountains; that would illustrate the intriguing juxtaposition of the three great lumber flumes; that would compare the various railroads, inclines, sawmills, and lumber camps; and that would—I hoped—preserve the flavor of a colorful bygone time in a single volume.

The majority of photographs accompanying the text have not been previously published. Those few that have are included because they have unique value to the story. Unless otherwise credited, all photographs are from my own collection.

I owe a great debt to the hundreds of considerate persons, many of whom have since passed on, who helped me over the years. Virtually all have been cited in previous acknowledgements; the list is far too long to repeat here. Valuable assistance on this specific book was graciously provided by Craig Konklin, Jim Law, Don DeVere, Bob Kimble, Harold Olson, Lewis Eaton, Doug Richter, and Harold Schutt. Material came from a wide variety of sources: library annals, newspaper files, government records, historical archives, private collections, and—to a great extent—the recollections of the erstwhile workaday loggers themselves. Their assistance and their friendship will always be remembered.

Here, then, is *The Whistles Blow No More*—the story of the six railroads that logged the southern Sierra Nevada during the Age of Steam. They spanned the era between the ox-drawn log cart and the diesel truck; between the long-handled ax and the two-man chain saw. No mountainside was too steep for their venturesome rails; no forest too remote; no trees too big.

Few remain who saw their passing. The show is too long over. But the impact of their flumes and rails on the history of central California will not soon be forgotten.

HANK JOHNSTON
Yosemite, California

This is a "picture tree" in Converse Basin. Extra-large undercuts were sometimes made in the giant Sequoia trees logged by the Sanger Lumber Company so loggers could pose for pictures when the photographer came around on Sunday. Photographs like this illustrate the enormous size of the great trees. (Harold Schutt Collection)

CHAPTER ONE

The Six Railroad Loggers—An Overview

THE SIERRA NEVADA mountains—"the most divinely beautiful of all the mountain chains"—stretch for more than 400 miles along the eastern edge of California like a great granite wall. The range, essentially one magnificent mountain 40 to 80 miles wide, is the highest and steepest in the contiguous 48 states. A dozen of its peaks tower over 14,000 feet above sea level; fully 500 exceed 12,000 feet.

The Sierra range was formed in prehistoric times by a massive upthrust that tilted a huge block of igneous granite toward the coast—thereby producing a short, precipitous descent into Owens Valley on the eastern side of the range, and a long, gradual slope into the gold country foothills on the west.

The abundant natural resources of the Sierra—water, timber, minerals, and scenery—played a salient role in California's dynamic but relatively belated development. The discovery of "placer gold" in the lower elevations of Sierran streams in 1848, for example, lured nearly 300,000 intrepid newcomers to California during the decade between 1850 and 1860—the largest and fastest mass migration in history.

The lumber needs of the booming new state were insatiable—for stores, for homes, for industries. The jerry-built city of San Francisco alone consumed uncounted millions of board feet between 1849 and 1851 when it burned down and was hastily rebuilt six times in a single 18-month period.

During the first few years of the gold rush, with only a handful of sawmills operating in all of California, lumber was largely imported from distant sources: Australia, China, Norway, and the northeastern United States. Enterprising New England ship captains, carrying gold seekers around Cape Horn to California, filled every available space with lumber, which they sold in San Francisco at huge profits.

By 1852, however, schooners plying Pacific Coast shipping lanes began arriving at California ports with load after load of "Oregon pine" (actually Douglas fir). The Oregon product quickly monopolized the market: in 1858, 95 percent of the 10 million board feet of lumber sold in Sacramento was redwood and "Oregon pine."

Ironically, the pristine forests of the nearby western Sierra—the finest forests of their kind in the world, according to John Muir—remained largely untouched by lumbermen. The rugged character of the roadless timber belt, with its myriad peaks and canyons, made profitable logging a practical impossibility. "Had the Sierra forests been cheaply accessible," Muir said, "the most valuable of them commercially would have fallen to the lumbermen. Thus far it costs less to go a thousand miles up the coast where the trees come down to the shores of navigable rivers and bays, than 50 miles up the mountains."

Small sawmills began cutting in the Sierra foothills before the Civil War, but the problem of getting lumber to city markets restricted sales to local mining camp customers. Freighting costs alone, from mountain mill to valley floor, often cost more than the Oregon products sold for in cargo lots in San Francisco. As a result, for many years most Sierra sawmills were rudimentary enterprises that lasted only until the surrounding timber had been exhausted.

Near the close of the last century, however, improved logging technology in the form of V-flumes, steam donkey engines, and geared railroad locomotives made large-scale mountain logging potentially profitable for the first time. Moreover, the completion of the new railroad system through the adjacent San Joaquin Valley offered easy access to nationwide markets.

In the 1870s and 1880s, professional lumber operators started scouting the Sierra forests in search of desirable stands to cut. Some were West Coast entrepreneurs; others came from the Lake states—Minnesota, Michigan, and Wisconsin—where the forests were fast reaching the level of depletion that had prompted lumbermen to abandon Maine 40 years earlier. During the next two decades, the well-financed newcomers acquired the rights to thousands upon thousands of acres of the finest timber in California. Some bought the land outright, usually at bargain prices. Others thriftily paid only for stumpage (the right to clear the timber). And a few unscrupulous operators covertly hired local hangers-

Logging in the Sierra before the advent of steam power was an awesome task. Here a young skid greaser prepares to start down an early skid road carrying a pail of grease. He will use the broom to spread the lubricant over the skids to ease the oxen's burden. (Harold Schutt Collection)

on from nearby towns for a few dollars each to file homestead or mining claims up to 160 acres on choice government forest areas, which were then illegally passed on to their employers.

The first logging venture of consequence in the southern Sierra was the California Lumber Company, incorporated in 1874 by a group of prominent San Joaquin Valley businessmen. The ambitious project comprised a two-saw circular steam sawmill set high in the mountains above present Oakhurst, and a 52-mile V-flume, by far the longest in the world at the time, to carry rough-cut lumber to a finishing mill at what became known as Madera in the San Joaquin Valley. The flume worked so successfully that lumber prices were soon reduced to about half the previous rate charged by competing mills using conventional overland transportation.

In 1877 a severe drought in the valley ruined the local market and forced the California Lumber Company into bankruptcy. Three years later, however, with the economy on the upswing, the firm's principal creditors reopened the operation under the name of the Madera Flume and Trading Company. The new organization immediately prospered. Over the next several years, two more sawmills were added to the mountain facilities, and in 1889 the Sierra's first logging railroad, a four-mile, narrow-gauge line powered by a diminutive 0-4-0 locomotive affectionately called *Betsy,* was built near Soquel Meadow. The MF&T closed down its mountain mills at the end of the 1892 season after cutting over most of its timber; by 1898 all business had been suspended.

In 1899 a successor corporation known as the Madera Sugar Pine Company was formed by MF&T officials Return Roberts and Elmer Cox in conjunction with a group of wealthy Michigan lumbermen who owned large tracts of choice timber adjoining the previous operation. The new corporation built a large sawmill—steam powered with a 72-inch carriage and two 60-inch circular saws—and an elaborate company town at a place called Sugar Pine, just south of Yosemite National Park. The old V-flume to Madera was rebuilt to the new mill site, extending its total length to 54 miles.

The second California mill of the Madera Flume and Trading Company appears to be rather undersized to handle the large redwood log on the wooden-wheeled wagon at right. This mill had a "dry landing" (no log pond).

During the next 32 seasons, the company averaged a yearly cut of some 40 million board feet, using seven locomotives, more than 100 log cars, and about 140 miles of railroad track in all. When the operation shut down at the end of the 1931 season, it had been the longest-lived and most profitable of all the Sierra railroad loggers.

Seeing the success of the Madera venture, two other fluming companies constructed extensive installations in the Sierra only a few miles to the south. In 1888 two West Coast lumbermen named Hiram Smith and Austin Moore incorporated the Kings River Lumber Company after acquiring some 30,000 acres of excellent timber near Sequoia National Park. Most of the property had been fraudulently obtained during the preceding several summers by hiring transients to file homestead claims, often on tracts they hadn't even seen, which were then promptly passed on to Smith and Moore. The U.S. Interior Department belatedly made a cursory investigation of the land grab but failed to take any formal action.

In 1889 the Kings River Lumber Company built two sawmills in the mountains at a place called Millwood, a 54-mile V-flume to Sanger in the San Joaquin Valley, and—two years later—a narrow-gauge logging railroad to reach outlying timber. Beset by financial problems almost from the beginning, the operation was reorganized as The Sanger Lumber Company by creditors in 1895. The new owners constructed a large band mill five miles to the east in the midst of a great stand of Sierra redwoods at Converse Basin, and during the next 10 years carried on the most destructive lumbering ever known in the world. Some 8,000 *Sequoia Gigantea,* the mightiest trees on earth (many exceeded 25 feet in diameter), were cut down to no one's benefit, as the company continued to lose money every season.

In 1905 the assets were sold to Michigan lumbermen Thomas Hume and Ira Bennett, and the mill, flume, and railroad moved four miles east to a new location called Hume Lake, in honor of the principal stockholder. Known first as the Hume-Bennett Lumber Company, and later as Sanger Lumber Company after Hume bought out Bennett's interest, the enterprise continued intermittent and unprofitable logging through 1923, when it shut down permanently. During its lifetime the operation averaged a yearly cut of 20 million board feet, using three locomotives, 50 log cars, and about 30 miles of track.

The third fluming installation, the Fresno Flume and Irrigation Company, began as a combination logging and irrigation undertaking. Incorporated in 1891 to succeed an earlier company by Fresno-area businessmen in partnership with C.B. Shaver and Lewis Swift, two experienced Michigan lumbermen, the firm erected a rock-fill dam across Stevenson Creek in the Sierra east of Fresno to form Shaver

The upper mill of the Sanger Lumber Company was one of two mills the company operated at Millwood. The various flume branches appearing above merged into a single unit below the mill to carry lumber down the 54-mile route to Sanger.

The huge pine log resting on the cart that carried logs from the lake to the entrance of the Shaver Lake mill is appropriately painted with the date (July 4, 1896) and the names of the holiday celebrants who pose here for the photographer.

Lake, which served as both a mill pond for log storage and the water supply for the flume. Then followed the building of a large double-circular, steam-powered sawmill adjoining the lake and a 45-mile flume to the newborn valley town of Clovis, where a finishing mill was established.

The flume had been originally planned as a double structure; V-shaped on top to float lumber to Clovis, and box-shaped part of the way underneath to transport water to the head of Big Dry Creek above Tollhouse. At this point water was to be dumped from the box flume into the natural channel of the creek bed and ultimately sold to farmers in the foothills and valley below. Lawsuits by owners of the riparian rights to San Joaquin River water in 1894 prevented this ideal arrangement, however, and caused a temporary injunction to be issued that stopped the lumber company from using any water at all. Fortunately for the Shaver interests, a compromise was reached whereby Fresno Flume was allowed to maintain its dam and lake but divert only enough water to float lumber to Clovis in the V-flume.

Logging started at Shaver in 1894 using solid-wheeled log wagons pulled by ox teams. Later, movable donkey engines snaked logs down chutes from the cutting areas to long, greased skidways, where larger bull engines pulled the logs to the lake. Here they were dumped into the water and towed in a boom by a small steamboat across the lake to the mill entrance. In 1902, as logging moved farther from the lake, the firm bought the first of two geared locomotives and eventually built about 12 miles of railroad track running to the south and east.

The company changed its name to the Fresno Flume and Lumber Company in 1908, in keeping with its real function. In 1912, several years after the death of both Swift and Shaver, the remaining stockholders sold out for almost a million dollars to Ira Bennett, a former principal in the nearby Hume-Bennett Lumber Company. Two years later a storm knocked down two miles of flume, which were never rebuilt. Bennett, who was in financial trouble at the time, ceased all logging at the end of 1914.

During its 21 seasons, the Fresno Flume and Lumber Company averaged a yearly cut of some 25 million board feet. Its overall success, along with that of the neighboring Madera Sugar Pine Company, demonstrated the practicality of the great V-flumes for lumber transport. In 1919 the Southern California Edison Company bought most of the Shaver property for addition to its expanding Big Creek hydroelectric project. Edison built a new dam in 1927, which created the present, greatly enlarged Shaver Lake.

About eight miles south of Shaver, the Pine Ridge Lumber Company, smallest and least known of the Sierra railroad loggers, owned 2,700 timbered acres and a double-circular steam sawmill along the banks of Rush Creek. The company was incorporated in 1899 to take over the assets of the firm of Smyth and McCardle, which had logged the property with ox teams since 1884. Herman Peterson, president of the new corporation and an experienced lumberman, had been an employee and later a partner in the earlier operation.

Although logging began on Pine Ridge in 1854, the difficulty of transporting lumber down the formidable Tollhouse Grade to valley markets plagued local lumbermen for many years. The construction of the Shaver Lake flume through the area in 1893 solved the delivery problem and caused a number of small sawmills to spring up on Pine Ridge in the late 1890s. Loggers hauled their lumber on wagons to a place on the Pine Ridge road called "the Saddle," where the flume paralleled the road. The flume company purchased the lumber at an agreed-on price in 4,000-foot bundles, placed it on skids, and when its own run from Shaver Lake had stopped for the day, sent the purchased lumber down to the finishing mill at Clovis. Some years the company bought almost as much lumber as it produced at its own sawmill.

The Pine Ridge Lumber Company was situated only six miles by rough road from the Saddle, and its entire output was sold to Fresno Flume and Lumber. In 1902, with the lumber market on the rise, Herman Peterson decided he needed a railroad to reach certain stands of fir, pine, and cedar some distance from the mill that were described as "among the largest and finest in the mountains." He soon

The sawmill of the Pine Ridge Lumber Company was supplied with logs by ox teams and wooden-wheeled wagons in pre-railroad days. This view shows the mill in 1890 when it was owned by Smyth and McCardle.

Locomotive No. 29 of the Yosemite Valley Railroad arrives at the Merced Falls sawmill of the Yosemite Lumber Company in the mid-1920s. The trainload of logs is from the lumber company's logging operations near Yosemite National Park.

purchased a new 15-ton, Class A Climax locomotive for the purpose, along with the hardware for six bobtailed log cars (the wooden frames were built at the site), and enough used 25-pound Fresno streetcar rail to lay three miles of standard-gauge track. The railroad main line eventually ran both north and south from the mill, crossing three trestles (one nearly 200 feet long) en route. In the woods, oxen—and later, two steam donkeys—brought logs to landings along the railroad where the three sets of tiny log cars were loaded. The wood-burning Climax made three round trips to the mill during each 11-hour workday.

Pine Ridge Lumber was a sound operation, employing about 50 men at peak times and averaging a yearly cut of nearly three million board feet. In the fall of 1912, however, the company's timber supply finally came to an end, and the sawmill was shut down for good. Peterson hauled his locomotive and cars a few miles up the road and worked under contract for a year helping to clear the basin that would soon be Huntington Lake, the first reservoir in the Big Creek hydroelectric system. He subsequently returned to the logging business, running sawmills in several California timber areas including Pine Ridge, but the ultimate fate of his unusual little Climax engine is unknown to this day.

The Yosemite Lumber Company was the only southern Sierra logger fortunate enough to be in proximity to a common carrier railroad—in this case the Yosemite Valley Railroad, which ran 78 miles from Merced to a terminus at El Portal just west of Yosemite Valley. Incorporated in 1910 by northern California lumber investors, the Yosemite Lumber

Company constructed the steepest logging incline ever known in 1912 from the Merced River Canyon straight up the mountain to the top of Henness Ridge 3,100 feet above. From the incline summit, the company built more than 30 miles of logging railroad into the woods, much of it within the boundaries of Yosemite National Park between Badger Pass and Wawona.

Although large-scale logging in a national park seems unthinkable today, Yosemite Lumber somehow acquired the right to log "dead and decaying timber" in Yosemite by means of two special acts of Congress in 1912 and 1914. The legislation gave the Secretary of the Interior absolute authority to dispose of any timber in the park that "he deemed advisable," in return for which the lumber company agreed to transfer to the government certain scenic strips bordering the old Wawona Road. Surprisingly, despite the protests of a few early conservationists, there seems to have been little public outcry about the unique situation, and the company cut some 200 million board feet of "dead and decaying timber" within the park over a period of several years.

In the forest, Yosemite Lumber employed both chutes and high-lead yarding sides to bring logs to its landings along the railroad. Geared locomotives and 174 bulkhead log cars then transported the log loads to the head of the incline. The five-foot-high bulkheads on the front of the cars kept logs from sliding forward as the cars were lowered one at a time down the steep incline tracks at the end of a thick steel cable. A huge steam hoist at the summit provided power for the incline setup, which is more fully described in a subsequent chapter.

Unlike the previous mountain logging operations, the Yosemite Lumber Company's sawmill was situated at the edge of the San Joaquin Valley in the town of Merced Falls, about 54 miles west of El Portal. Log trains, made up at the foot of the incline, were hauled to the mill pond at Merced Falls by Yosemite Valley Railroad locomotives.

After 12 moderately successful seasons, Yosemite Lumber ran out of timber on the south side of the Merced River. In 1924 logging moved to the north side of the canyon, and a new incline was constructed from the Merced River to a point near the top of Trumbull Peak, about five miles west of the first incline. From the hoist location at the top, the logging railroad took off into the forest as before.

During the ensuing six years, the company's fortunes underwent a series of ups and downs, ranging from its largest yearly cut of 85 million board feet in 1925 to the suspension of all operations in 1931 fol-

The breathtaking descent of the first big incline of the Yosemite Lumber Company, running down from Henness Ridge to El Portal, is quite evident in this early photograph. (James Law Collection)

lowing a change of ownership. After four years of inaction, the operation was reorganized in 1935 as the Yosemite Sugar Pine Lumber Company with John Ball, an executive of White and Friant, owners of much of the remaining timber, as president. Logging resumed in the woods and the new enterprise appeared to be prospering, when the federal government condemned 7,200 acres of the company's finest sugar pine property for addition to Yosemite National Park in 1939. The forced sale reduced Yosemite Lumber's available timber by such an extent that the company closed down for good at the end of the 1942 season.

The Yosemite Lumber Company averaged a yearly cut of 55 million board feet during its lengthy lifetime, running five locomotives over nearly a hundred miles of track. The most volatile of the Sierra railroad logging operations, it achieved both high profits and deep losses at various times over the years, depending largely on the management and the economy at any given time. The company's premature closure in 1942 played a major role in the Yosemite Valley Railroad's untimely demise only three years later.

The last railroad logging operation to be built in the southern Sierra was perhaps the most lamentable failure in the history of American lumbering. Incorporated in 1921 as the Sugar Pine Lumber Company, the enterprise went bankrupt after only nine seasons despite having the finest logging facilities in the West.

Sugar Pine Lumber's principal owner was Arthur

The first trainload of logs for the giant four-band sawmill of the Sugar Pine Lumber Company at Pinedale stands at the log pond on July 12, 1923.

Fleming, a millionaire lawyer from Michigan by way of Pasadena, who had inherited a minority share in the Madera Sugar Pine Company some years before. Encouraged by the success of that venture, Fleming invested his personal fortune of nearly $5 million, along with another $5 million of his daughter's funds that he was administering at the time, in the ill-fated Sugar Pine Lumber undertaking.

In 1922-23 the company constructed: (1) A huge four-band sawmill and company town at Pinedale in the San Joaquin Valley near Fresno; (2) the most modern lumber camp of its time high in the Sierra above Bass Lake with hotel-type housing for 500 lumberjacks; and (3) 64 miles of first-class standard-gauge railroad to deliver logs from woods to mill by means of 10 locomotives and 220 cars. In the mountains, about 150 miles of logging railroad spread out into the forest surrounding Central Camp, the mountain headquarters. At the various logging sides, multi-drum electric yarders hauled logs to landings along the railroad using towering high-lead and skyline rig-ups. Power was supplied to the unusual machines—specially made by the Willamette Iron and Steel Company—over miles of high-voltage cable strung through the woods.

Start-up costs of the elaborate complex, which exceeded $10 million, left the corporation short of working capital from the outset, and continued mismanagement exacerbated the already tenuous situation. In spite of an average yearly cut in excess of 100 million board feet during six of its seven seasons of full operation (including the Sierra's all-time record production of 117 million board feet in 1926), the Sugar Pine Lumber Company lost money every year of its corporate life.

By the fall of the depression year of 1931, Arthur Fleming had finally exhausted his resources. With unsold lumber piled high in the drying yards, the big Pinedale mill closed down never to reopen. Two years later, the principal creditors took over the bankrupt corporation's physical assets, scrapped the railroad, and gradually disposed of the real estate and equipment piecemeal at a fraction of their original cost. It was an ignominious end to "Fleming's Folly"—surely the most flamboyant fiasco in steam-logging history.

Because the railroad logging era spanned more than half a century, the six southern Sierra operations were never all in business at the same time. In 1912, however, five of the six companies simultaneously worked the mountain slopes, and four were in concurrent production during 15 other seasons. All but the Sugar Pine Lumber Company had several names, owners, or locations at various times over the years. Yet they were always basically a continuation of the same operation, using the same employees and equipment. To minimize confusion in the material that follows, the most identifiable company name is applied throughout in general reference; in a few specific instances involving a particular place or event, the name given is the one in use by the company at the time.

THE RAILROAD LOGGERS: A Corporate History

■

MADERA SUGAR PINE COMPANY
Madera, California • Operated 1899–1932

Incorporated May 8, 1899, by Arthur Hill, Elmer Cox, Return Roberts, and E.M. Fowler. Successors to the Madera Flume and Trading Company, incorporated May 21, 1878, by Edward McLaughlin, Caius Ryland, Mariano Malarin, Return Roberts, and William Kelley. Successors to the California Lumber Company, incorporated February 8, 1874, by P.D. Wigginton, Mark Howell, William Thurman, James Dickinson, *et al.*

SANGER LUMBER COMPANY
Sanger, California • Operated 1889–1923

Incorporated January 24, 1917, by name-change amendment from Hume-Bennett Lumber Company. Hume-Bennett Lumber Company, incorporated November 22, 1905, by Thomas Hume, Ira Bennett, George Hefferan, and George Hume. Successors to The Sanger Lumber Company, incorporated October 15, 1894, by A.D. Moore, Walter Young, Ivory Littlefield, H.C. Smith, and Charles Johnson. Successors to the Kings River Lumber Company, incorporated April 24, 1888, by Austin D. Moore, Hiram Smith, John Hanify, Alonzo Grim, and John Jarboe.

FRESNO FLUME AND LUMBER COMPANY
Clovis, California • Operated 1893–1914

Incorporated December 13, 1912, by Ira Bennett, F.L. Bennett, and J.G. Ferguson. Successors to the Fresno Flume and Lumber Company, incorporated September 8, 1908, by name-change amendment from Fresno Flume and Irrigation Company. Fresno Flume and Irrigation Company, incorporated October 31, 1891, by F. Bullard, J.M. Heiskell, D.C. Sample, H.L. Musick, *et al.* (Reorganized in 1892 by C.B. Shaver, R.B. Butler, H.L. Musick, L.P. Swift, and H.D. Colson.) Successors to the Big Dry Creek Flume Company, incorporated April 18, 1890, by J.M. Heiskell, D.C. Sample, F.F. Letcher, L.J. Miller, and C.D. Davis.

PINE RIDGE LUMBER COMPANY
Fresno, California • Operated 1900–1912

Incorporated November 25, 1899, by Herman Peterson, Rose Peterson, J.H. Shadle, J.F. Rouch, and W.H. McKenzie. Successors to (John) Smyth and (James) McCardle, a partnership formed in 1884 (Smyth's interest taken over by Herman Peterson and J.F. Rouch in 1893). Successors to Mose Mock, who built the original mill in 1883.

YOSEMITE SUGAR PINE LUMBER COMPANY
Merced Falls, California • Operated 1912–1942

Incorporated July 15, 1935, by John Ball, Tom Ware, and Frank Lee. Successors to the Yosemite Lumber Company, incorporated May 1929, by Arthur Fleming, Robert Gillis, and James Clifford. Successors to the Yosemite Lumber Company incorporated May 1913, by James Tyson, F.M. Fenwick, Frank Drumm, E.H. Cox, *et al.* Successors to the Yosemite Lumber Company incorporated August 1910, by James Tyson, F.M. Fenwick, Charles Nelson, *et al.*

SUGAR PINE LUMBER COMPANY
Pinedale, California • Operated 1923–1932

Incorporated July 26, 1921, by Arthur Fleming, Elmer Cox, Robert Gillis, and John Hemphill. Affiliated with the Minarets and Western Railway, incorporated March 19, 1921, by the same group of directors.

CHAPTER TWO

Sawmills of Every Description

THE SAW WAS KNOWN to the ancient Greeks, who deified its inventor, and the genealogy of the sawmill reaches back to at least the 14th century. Historical records show that from time to time during the next two or three centuries, sawmills were built in Germany, France, Norway, and the Netherlands. The first sawmill in America appears to have been built by Dutch millwrights at the Jamestown settlement in Virginia in the early 1600s. From this beginning, the lumber industry not only grew with the country, it helped the country to grow.

Early American mills were mostly small affairs of limited capacity, almost universally water-driven and of the "sash-saw" type. The sash saw was an ingenious device with a single saw blade held rigidly in a vertical frame or sash that moved with an up-and-down motion. The log was forced against the saw by a primitive form of ratchet feed works, and slowly sliced into boards. This represented some improvement over the old-style "pit sawing" in which the log was converted into boards by means of a long saw in the hands of two men, one on a platform above the log and one in a pit dug beneath it, but not much. The best output of a typical sash-saw mill was about 500 board feet per day.

The invention of the circular saw in the early 1800s marked the first real advancement in lumber-manufacturing equipment. As its name indicates, a circular saw is a large steel disk that substituted the entirely new principle of continuous motion. By about 1860, the faster and more efficient circular saw began gradually replacing the old up-and-down mills throughout the West.

Double-circular saw of the Fresno Flume and Lumber Company turned nearly a half inch of wood into sawdust with each cut. It was later replaced with a more efficient band saw.

But the depth of a circular saw's cut was necessarily limited to its radius. In the 1870s, the development of the double-circular saw—with one blade set above another—enabled mills to saw all but the largest logs into boards of any desired thickness by making simultaneous cuts in a log carried back and forth on an adjustable carriage.

The band saw was invented in England in 1808, but it was more than 75 years before American lumbermen began to make general use of band mills. A band sawmill consists essentially of two large steel wheels around which the endless toothed steel band revolves at a speed of some 10,000 feet a minute in the manner of a belt on pulleys. By the early 1900s the band saw, which could reduce even the great Sierra redwoods to planks, had become the favored equipment in all but the smallest sawmills.

The southern Sierra railroad loggers built 16 different sawmills over the years, and they were as diverse as the operations themselves. The huge four-band mill of the Sugar Pine Lumber Company at Pinedale, for example, with a capacity of 600,000 board feet a day, produced nearly as much lumber in just two 10-hour shifts as the tiny Pine Ridge Lumber Company's double-circular mill could turn out in a month.

Four of the six Sierra loggers—Sugar Pine Lumber, Fresno Flume and Lumber, Pine Ridge Lumber, and Yosemite Lumber—used the same basic mill structures throughout their existence. The Madera Sugar Pine Company (and its predecessors) had five sawmills, and the Sanger Lumber Company built seven mills in all. The first three Madera mills, operating in pre-railroad days, needed to be close to the cutting areas, which caused frequent changes of locale. The original Madera Sugar Pine mill at Sugar Pine burned to the ground in 1922 and was rebuilt the following spring. The Sanger Lumber Company's seven different mills were the result of several shifts in logging sites over the years and two disastrous fires.

The Sugar Pine Lumber Company and the Yosemite Lumber Company were the only two southern Sierra loggers to locate their sawmills out of the mountains. As previously mentioned, the Yosemite Lumber Company had the good fortune to be able to hire the common carrier Yosemite Valley Railroad to deliver its logs to the mill pond at Merced Falls. Here the company owned a modern two-band mill, built in 1911–12 and enlarged in 1923, that served it well for 30 years. The Sugar Pine Lumber Company mill, built at Pinedale on 574 acres in 1922–23, consisted of 15 structures covering more than 14 acres of floor area. The all-electric layout was considered the most modern in America at the time.

The three fluming operations—Madera Sugar Pine, Fresno Flume and Lumber, and Sanger Lumber—which had their sawmills in the timber belt, had the advantage of leaving all residue close to the logging sites. Only rough-sawn lumber was shipped out of the mountains to the planing mill and drying yard at each flume terminus in the San Joaquin Valley. The planing mills also had fire problems; the Madera Flume and Trading Company yard at Madera burned to the ground in 1881, and the Fresno Flume and Irrigation facility at Clovis was leveled by fire in 1898. Both were promptly rebuilt.

The southern Sierra railroad loggers cut nearly five billion board feet of lumber over the years. The approximate total production of each operation was: Madera Sugar Pine Company, 1½ billion board feet; Yosemite Lumber Company, 1⅓ billion board feet; Sugar Pine Lumber Company, 800 million board feet; Sanger Lumber Company, 540 million board feet; Fresno Flume and Lumber Company, 450 million board feet; and Pine Ridge Lumber Company, 60 million feet.

Today, aside from a few crumbling foundations, there is little left to mark the sites of the 16 assorted sawmills that performed so efficiently during the Age of Steam. More than 40 years have passed since the last log went through the last sawmill, and only the photographs remain to show us how it used to be. Here are some of them.

The log carriage inside the Shaver Lake mill of the Fresno Flume and Lumber Company as it looked after the installation of the band saw in the early 1900s.

Logs ride the endless-chain conveyor of the Yosemite Lumber Company's mill at Merced Falls. Note the bark-washing spray.

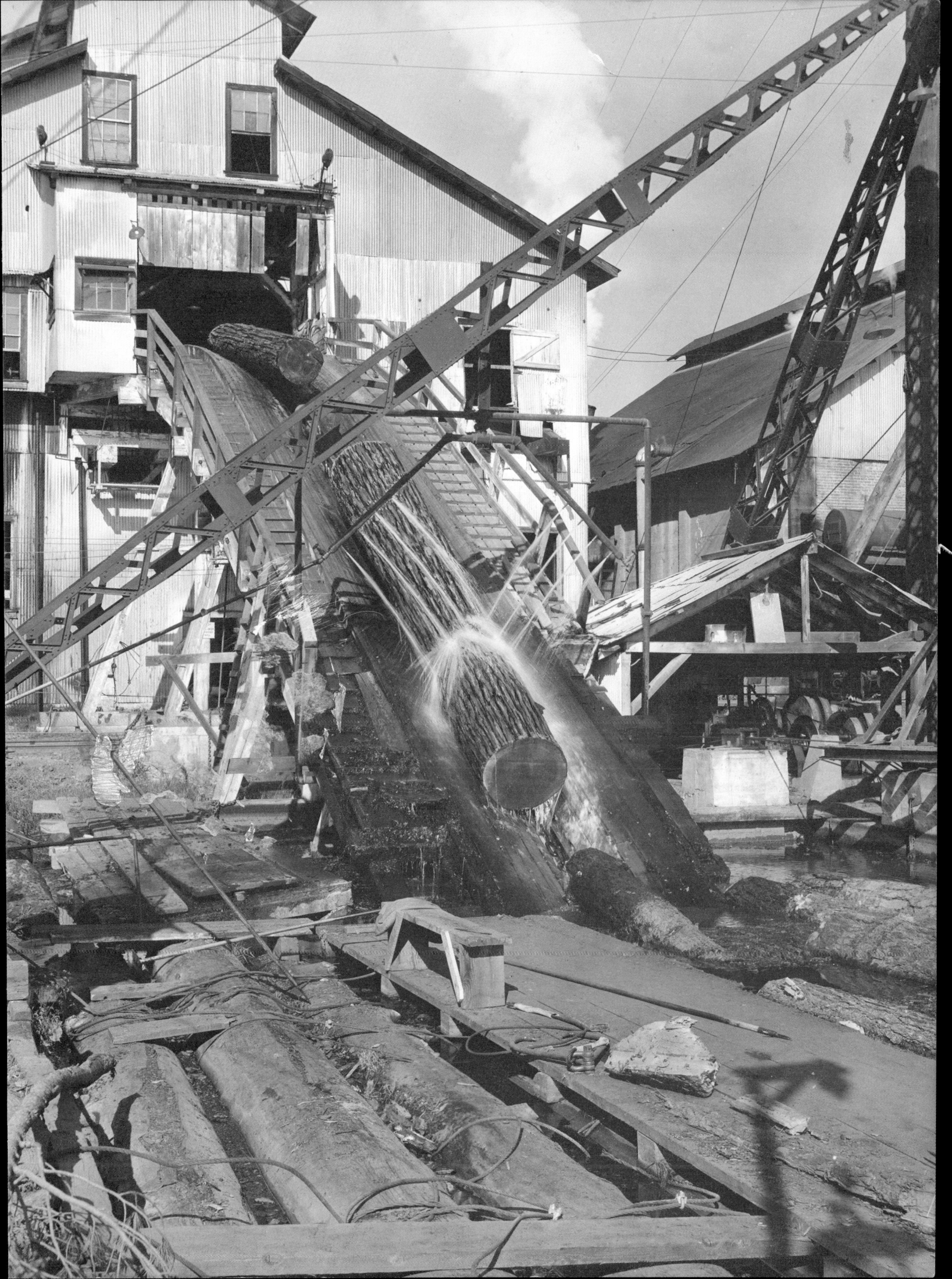

The second sawmill of the Sanger Lumber Company in Converse Basin as photographed shortly after construction in 1906 (the original mill burned down). The new mill had a daily capacity of 175,000 board feet.

Shaver Lake

A rock quarry adjoining the Shaver Lake Dam **(above)** supplied material for the rock-fill structure, which was 50 feet high from the bottom and 90 feet wide. The lake created was three miles long, with an average depth of 10 feet.

The mill was framed and the boilers set in this construction scene **(left)** taken in the early summer of 1893. A few weeks later the crew watched **(opposite, top)** as the big smokestack was hoisted into position.

The completed mill and lake looked like this about 1900 **(opposite, bottom).**

Log Ponds

The Madera Sugar Pine Company's unloading rig at Sugar Pine **(above)** was steam-powered from the mill system. The boom at right was used to raise sinkers, which were usually the butt logs from sugar pine or white fir trees.

The Sugar Pine Lumber Company's log dump at Pinedale **(left)** used twin electric hoists to unload two cars simultaneously. The company handled more than 13,000 carloads of logs each season at its height (average load: eight logs totaling 7,500 feet of lumber). It took less than one minute per car to unload a train.

At the Hume Lake mill of the Sanger Lumber Company, an A-frame hoist unloaded cars from a trestle extending along the lake edge.

The log dump at Shaver Lake was similar to the Hume facility. A steam-powered boom tipped logs off cars that had been pushed out on a trestle over the lake.

Here is another view of a Madera Sugar Pine log train at the unloading ramp at Sugar Pine. A pond tender rides a raft at the left.

These pictures illustrate some of the diverse methods used to transport logs from pond to mill. Two stages of operation at Sugar Pine: a log enters the mill on a cart in 1905 **(opposite, bottom)**; another log approaches the same position in 1930 **(above)**, after the addition of a pressure spray.

Log cart at Hume Lake **(left)** conveys a good-sized stick to the head rig.

The arrangement at Shaver Lake **(below)** was the same type as the ones at Hume and Sugar Pine. Logs were floated onto a submerged cart, which was then pulled up a ramp on a track to the mill entrance.

Logs were carried from the pond to the four-band sawmill of the Sugar Pine Lumber Company at Pinedale **(opposite, top)** by this endless-chain conveyor.

NO SMOKING.

Clovis Planing Mill

The box factory and planing mill of the Fresno Flume and Lumber Company at Clovis burned to the ground in 1898 on the very day the insurance expired. The local agent's oral commitment of renewal to the owners was honored by the insurance company, however, and the plant was soon rebuilt. The original mill is shown **(above)** in the mid-1890s.

Once the fire began **(left)** the smoke and flames were so intense that firefighters could do little more than watch the conflagration. The new mill, erected after the fire **(right)** was larger and better equipped than the previous facility. (Lewis Eaton Collection)

The Saw Filers

Keeping the big band saws sharp was a full-time occupation for the saw filers, who were usually situated in a garret above the main mill floor. Because each band ordinarily used four saws daily, a stock of four or five saws was kept on hand for each band. The saw-filing room of the Yosemite Lumber Company at Merced Falls **(left)** utilized the most modern equipment then available.

Filers at the Converse Basin mill of the Sanger Lumber Company **(below)** were kept busy sharpening the two small band saws and the big redwood splitter used in the mill.

Log Storage

At the Fresno Flume and Lumber Company's mountain logging operations at Shaver Lake, logs were dumped into the water on the opposite side of the lake from the mill. A small steamboat called the *Michigan* then pulled the logs in a large boom across the lake to the sawmill area **(right).** Here they were held in storage until needed.

The log-storage pond of the Madera Sugar Pine Company **(below)** held a ''full deck'' in this photograph taken in the early 1900s. The railroad unloading track can be seen running along the left edge of the pond.

The Giant Splitter

Cutting the great redwood logs at the Sanger Lumber Company's Converse Basin mill was accomplished in later years by the use of this special 86-foot band saw. Called the ''longest saw in the world'' at the time, the lengthy ribbon of steel eliminated some of the waste previously caused by blowing the big logs apart with dynamite.

These two views of the Yosemite Lumber Company's sawmill at Merced Falls show the steam drag saw **(above)** that was used to cut logs to proper lengths before they entered the band mill, and **(below)** the small band head rig inside the mill.

Sawmill Construction

Building a sawmill in the San Joaquin Valley was a far easier task than a similar project in the mountains of the Sierra. The Yosemite Lumber Company mill at Merced Falls, which stood alongside the right-of-way of the Yosemite Valley Railroad, is pictured under construction in 1912 **(opposite, top)** and in later operation **(opposite, bottom).**

All equipment for the Sanger Lumber Company mill at Hume Lake had to be transported by mule-drawn wagons over crude roads built for the purpose. The construction scene of the Hume mill **(right)** was taken on April 11, 1908. The unusual multiple-arch dam and finished mill are shown **(below)** about 1910.

Sunday in the Sierra

The first Converse Basin mill of the Sanger Lumber Company nears completion in this 1897 scene.

BASIN, CAL.

Contrasts

The large and small of southern Sierra railroad logging were the great four-band mill of the Sugar Pine Lumber Company at Pinedale **(above)** and the tiny circular mill of the Pine Ridge Lumber Company near Shaver Lake **(left).** The Pine Ridge outfit's entire railroad roster can be seen here: three sets of logging disconnects and one Class A Climax locomotive.

The lower mill of the Sanger Lumber Company was situated about two miles below Millwood. Shay locomotive No. 1 has just pulled alongside the dry rollway area at left with a load of logs for the mill in this 1891 photograph. The railroad was moved to the upper mill by 1893, but the lower mill continued to operate until 1896, using a network of feeder chutes.

Sanger Lumber Company's No. 1, the *Sequoia,* pauses for the photographer on one of the 23 trestles on the railroad that ran some six miles between Millwood and Hoist Ridge. The cars are laden with lumber from the Converse Basin mill. The boards will be flumed to Sanger after the load reaches its destination at Millwood.

CHAPTER THREE

Railroads in the Woods

WORKING ON A LOGGING RAILROAD in the Sierra Nevada was not the easiest way to earn a living. The track was light, the curves were tight, and the grades would have challenged a mountain goat. The job was to bring logs to the sawmill from timber-cutting sites as quickly and cheaply as possible.

The battered second- and third-hand rails of the Sierra logging railroads wound through some of the most beautiful scenery in America, yet danger stalked every mile of the way in the form of wrecks, washouts, and derailments. There were snowstorms in the spring, rainstorms in the fall, and the constant peril of fire. Hauling a trainload of groaning, overburdened log cars across a spindly wooden trestle, sometimes a hundred feet in the air, was not a task for the faint-hearted. The country seemed to be "standing on end," and a stretch of level right-of-way in the Sierra was harder to find than a pretty woman.

Exactly when and where the first locomotive hauled the first load of logs out of the woods will probably never be known. Some historians say it occurred as early as 1852 in New York State; others name Michigan, Pennsylvania, or Georgia as the site of the epoch-making event. In any case, by the early 1870s logging railroads were operating in many parts of the United States. Laid in a variety of gauges, they had one thing in common: crude wooden rails fashioned from poles or stringers, sometimes topped with scrap iron to prevent excessive wear.

The first logging railroad to use steel rails was built in Michigan in 1876. A second railroad followed a year later, and by 1885 49 logging lines were operating in Michigan alone.

Early logging railroads had only rod locomotives available for motive power—usually small industrial engines or high-wheeled castoffs from main-line service. Their effectiveness was extremely limited in mountainous timber country. The wheels spun under heavy loads, and on grades of even two or three percent the locomotives lost traction altogether.

In the late 1870s, however, a bearded, jack-of-all-trades lumberman from Michigan named Ephraim Shay pioneered a radical new type of locomotive that would soon revolutionize the logging business. Shay's story has been told many times, but simply put, his central idea incorporated the use of reducing gears instead of side rods, which gave his lopsided little locomotive—really little more than a vertical steam boiler set on an ordinary flat car—unheard-of tractive power. Every wheel on a Shay was a driving wheel, and—locked in their gears—the wheels could not spin. The locomotive's relatively light weight and maneuverability in proportion to its pulling power made it ideal for logging railroads where uncertain roadbed, steep grades, and heavy loads were the norm.

Shay entered into a licensing agreement with the Lima Machine Works of Lima, Ohio, which produced the first factory-built model in 1880. Despite later competition from other geared engines, notably the Climax and the Heisler, Shays soon became a fixture on logging and mining railroads all over the world.

The southern Sierra Nevada was no exception. Of the 28 locomotives on the six logging-company rosters over the years, only 22 actually worked the log spurs, and 16 of these were Lima Shays. The other logging engines consisted of four Mikado-type sad-

The 2-spot Shay of the Sanger Lumber Company pictured near Hume Lake in 1911.

Pine Ridge

The unusual Class A Climax of the Pine Ridge Lumber Company was a standard-gauge wood-burner. The two occupants of the locomotive **(facing page)** were obviously not the regular engineer and fireman.

The Climax crosses one of the three trestles on the three-mile line **(right).** This 150-foot trestle bridged a dry gulch about a mile north of the mill.

dle-tankers made by the American Locomotive Company and used in the woods by the Sugar Pine Lumber Company; the little Class A Climax of the Pine Ridge Lumber Company; and *Betsy,* Madera Sugar Pine's cog-geared engine previously mentioned as the first locomotive in the Sierra.

The remaining six locomotives comprised the four Mikados that plied the Sugar Pine Lumber Company's Minarets and Western main line from the Pinedale mill to Central Camp; a huge 2-10-2 saddle-tanker, also operated by SPL, mainly to help the Mikados pull empties back up the 4½ percent grade from Bass Lake to Central Camp; and a gas-mechanical Plymouth that Madera Sugar Pine bought in 1927 for ballasting and switching.

Part of the Sugar Pine Lumber Company's financial problems were apparently brought on by its use of Alco's saddle-tankers instead of Shays in the woods, according to an outside logging expert who was hired to analyze the operation in 1926. "The lumbering railroad, and especially the many spur lines, is on entirely too high a scale of excellence," the expert's report said. "The saddle-tank locomotives should be replaced by geared engines in the woods, which can negotiate sharper curves with lighter roadbed." SPL bought its only Shay soon after (1926) but used it mainly as a work-train engine. Meanwhile, the four Alco 2-8-2's continued as the principal motive power on the logging railroad, and the company continued to lose money every season.

Of the 22 locomotives employed in the woods, 12 burned cordwood and 10 burned fuel oil. Not surprisingly, the 12 wood-burners were all owned by the four flume companies whose only way of obtaining supplies at their remote mountain mills was by team and wagon from the distant San Joaquin Valley—a slow and expensive procedure. Wood, on the other hand, was obviously plentiful at the site. The two companies with direct rail connections with the outside world, Yosemite Lumber and Sugar Pine Lumber, brought in tank cars filled with fuel oil for their railroad equipment. Oil was easier to handle and rendered the average locomotive more efficient than when wood was burned.

The six loggers built nearly 500 miles of track during their 53-year run. Except for the Sugar Pine Lumber Company's main-line run from Central Camp to Pinedale, however, only a small portion of each company's total trackage was ever in use at any one time. As with most logging operations, spurs were laid into timber pockets, then torn up after the area was cut over and moved to another location. The same rail was sometimes used half-a-dozen times over a period of years.

Although narrow-gauge railroads could generally be constructed for less money than standard gauge, Madera Sugar Pine and Sanger Lumber were the only narrow-gauge logging lines in the southern Sierra. Perhaps the size of the timber was a determining factor, for Sanger Lumber converted its equipment and track to standard gauge in 1914 to better handle the large redwoods it was cutting at the time. Yosemite Lumber and Sugar Pine Lumber had no alternative to standard gauge because of their connections with main-line haulers en route to the mill (SPL ran over a portion of the Southern Pacific near Pinedale.)

The following rosters give the basic facts about all 28 southern Sierra locomotives. The data, arranged in columns, are (left to right): road number; type of engine; wheel size in inches including tire; cylinder diameter and piston stroke in inches; weight in pounds in normal operating condition; boiler pressure (pounds per square inch); tractive effort in pounds; builder; builder's number; and date built. Notes about individual locomotives and their disposition follow each tabular listing. Other information on the various railroads and equipment is provided in the photographic section that follows.

■

PINE RIDGE LUMBER COMPANY

(Standard Gauge, 1902–1912)

No. 1	**Class A**	**26**	**7 x 7**	**30,000**	**150**	**13,200**	**Climax**	**283**	**1901**

Purchased new. Used on Big Creek construction job, 1912–13. Possibly sold to the North Coast Lumber Company at Fort Ross, California.

FRESNO FLUME AND LUMBER COMPANY

(Standard Gauge, 1902–1914)

No. 1	**2T Shay**	**28**	**10 x 10**	**72,000**	**180**	**14,180**	**Lima**	**711**	**1902**
No. 2	**2T Shay**	**29½**	**10 x 12**	**84,000**	**180**	**16,900**	**Lima**	**2461**	**1911**

1. *Sierra* purchased new. Sold to Shaver Lake Lumber Company 8-19. Leased to Southern California Edison Company 8-19 to 1-26. Converted to oil by Edison. Sold to San Joaquin and Eastern for $2,333 at Cascada 1-26. Became SJ & E No. 1. Sold Liberman-Rosencrantz (D), Oakland, California, 8-33. Scrapped 1933.

2. Purchased new. Sold to Shaver Lake Lumber Company 8-19. Leased to Southern California Edison Company 8-19 to 1-26. Converted to oil by Edison. Sold to San Joaquin and Eastern for $3,419 at Cascada 1-26. Became SJ & E No. 2. Sold to Santa Cruz Lumber Company, Boulder Creek, California, for $2,375 3-30. Became Santa Cruz Lumber No. 1. Scrapped 1954.

YOSEMITE LUMBER COMPANY

(Standard Gauge, 1912–1942)

No. 1	**2T Shay**	**29½**	**10 x 12**	**84,000**	**180**	**20,840**	**Lima**	**2524**	**1912**
No. 2	**3T Shay**	**32**	**11 x 12**	**122,400**	**200**	**25,830**	**Lima**	**2660**	**1913**
No. 3	**3T Shay**	**36**	**12 x 15**	**146,000**	**200**	**34,000**	**Lima**	**2803**	**1915**
No. 4	**3T Shay**	**36**	**12 x 15**	**164,100**	**200**	**34,000**	**Lima**	**3092**	**1920**
No. 5	**3T Shay**	**36**	**12 x 15**	**174,700**	**200**	**30,350**	**Lima**	**3263**	**1924**

1. Purchased new. Partly destroyed by fire in 1940. Rebuilt as Yosemite Sugar Pine Lumber Company No. 6. Sold Davidson Company (D) 2-43. Scrapped 1947.

2. Purchased new. Sold Davidson Company (D) 2-43. Scrapped 4-47.

3. Purchased new. Sold Davidson Company (D) 3-43. Scrapped 4-47.

4. Purchased new. Sold Davidson Company (D) 5-43. Became Levin Metals and Steel Corporation (D). Sold Heeber Creeper (tourist) near Salt Lake City, Utah, 1971.

5. Ex-Mount Shasta Power Company No. 5, Bartle, California. Became Pacific Gas and Electric Company No. 5, Bartle, California. Purchased by YSPL Co. 1930, No. 5. Sold Davidson Company (D) 5-43. Sold Northern Redwood Lumber Company, Korbel, California No. 5, 1-45. Sold Simpson Redwood Lumber Company, 1957, No. 5. Sold Learner Steel Company (D), Oakland, California, 1957. Scrapped 1957.

MADERA SUGAR PINE COMPANY

(Standard Gauge, 1889–1931)

No. 1	**0-4-OT**			**14,000**				
No. 2	**2T Shay**	**29½**	**10 x 12**	**76,000**	**180**	**16,900**	**Lima 755**	**1902**
No. 3	**2T Shay**	**29½**	**10 x 12**	**76,000**	**180**	**16,900**	**Lima 862**	**1904**
No. 4	**2T Shay**	**29½**	**10 x 12**	**84,000**	**200**	**23,100**	**Lima 2280**	**1910**
No. 5	**3T Shay**	**32**	**11 x 12**	**120,000**	**200**	**25,830**	**Lima 2617**	**1912**
No. 6	**3T Shay**	**32**	**11 x 12**	**135,500**	**200**	**25,830**	**Lima 3306**	**1927**
No. 7	**Gas Mechanical, 4 wheel, 20 ton, built by Plymouth**							**1927**

1. *Betsy* purchased 1899 from Madera Flume and Trading Company. May have been built by Rose and Company, San Francisco. Scrapped 1937.
2. *Arthur Hill* purchased new. Scrapped 1937.
3. *E.M. Fowler* purchased new. Scrapped 1937.
4. *E.N. Briggs* purchased new. Scrapped 1937.
5. Purchased new. Sold Diamond and Caldor, Diamond Springs, California, for parts in 1937 for $500. Scrapped.
6. Purchased new. Sold Feather River Lumber Company, Delleker, California, for $3,000 11-35. Converted to oil. Became FRLC No. 6. Sold Hyman-Michaels Company (D), San Francisco, California, 1943. Sold Michigan-California Lumber Company (3rd No. 6), Camino, California, 6-44. Sold Hyman-Michaels Company (D), San Francisco, California, 1951. Scrapped 6-51.
7. Purchased new. Sold Grants Gravel Company, Friant, California, and converted to standard gauge.

SANGER LUMBER COMPANY

(Standard and Narrow Gauge, 1891–1923)

No. 1	**2T Shay**	**28**	**10 x 10**	**60,000**	**160**	**14,450**	**Lima**	**350**	**1891**
No. 2	**2T Shay**	**29**	**8 x 12**	**65,000**	**160**	**14,600**	**Lima**	**2411**	**1911**
No. 3	**2T Shay**	**29**	**8 x 12**	**65,000**	**160**	**14,600**	**Lima**	**2848**	**1916**

1. *Sequoia* purchased new by Kings River Lumber Company. Converted to standard gauge 1914. Sold to E.M. Prescott, Fresno, California, 1929. Scrapped.
2. Purchased new. Converted to standard gauge 1914. Sold to E.M. Prescott, Fresno, California, 1929. Boiler used by Byles-Jamison Lumber Company, Fresno, California, 1931–35, then Valley Paving Company, Fresno, California. Scrapped totally after 1945.
3. Purchased new (standard gauge). Sold E.M. Prescott, Fresno, California, 1929. Disposition unknown; may have run in the Philippines.

SUGAR PINE LUMBER COMPANY

(Standard Gauge, 1923–1931)

No. 1	**2-8-2T**	**44**	**20 x 24**	**190,000**	**190**	**35,200**	**Alco 64147**	**1923**
No. 2	**2-8-2T**	**44**	**20 x 24**	**190,000**	**190**	**35,200**	**Alco 64148**	**1923**
No. 3	**2-8-2T**	**44**	**20 x 24**	**188,500**	**190**	**35,200**	**Alco 65378**	**1924**
No. 4	**2-8-2T**	**44**	**20 x 24**	**197,500**	**190**	**35,200**	**Alco 66033**	**1925**
No. 5	**2-10-2T**	**48**	**22 x 28**	**267,500**	**220**	**52,800**	**Alco 67371**	**1927**
No. 10	**2T Shay**	**36**	**12 x 12**	**152,300**	**200**	**24,000**	**Lima 3301**	**1926**

1. Purchased new. Sold Pensacola Company, Los Angeles, California, 11-35. Sold Willamette Valley Lumber Company (2nd No. 1). Out of service 1944. Scrapped 1955.
2. Purchased new. Sold Pensacola Company, Los Angeles, California, 11-35. Sold Clark and Wilson Lumber Company, No. 16. Used on Portland and Southwestern Railway, No. 16. Scrapped 1955.
3. Purchased new. Sold Pensacola Company, Los Angeles, California, 11-35. Sold Flora Logging Company, No. 3, 1936. Sold Consolidated Timber Company, 2nd No. 2, 1939. Sold Kern and Kibbe Contracting Company, No. 2, 1945. Sold the Medford Corporation, No. 6. Rebuilt to 2-8-2; scrapped 6-52.
4. Purchased new. Sold Pensacola Company, Los Angeles, California, 11-35. Sold Pacific Lumber Company, No. 37. Sold railfan Frank Bayliss, No. 37, 1966. Sold Wawa and Concordville Inc., No. 37, 1966. Sold Wilmington and Western Railroad, No. 37 (tourist). Stored Chester, Pennsylvania.
5. Purchased new. Sold Pensacola Company, Los Angeles, California, 11-35. Sold Mason-Walsh-Atkinson-Kier Company, No. 800. Sold Consolidated Builders, Inc., No. 800. Sold H.J. Kaiser Company, No. 1119. Scrapped 1947.
10. Purchased new. Sold Pensacola Company, Los Angeles, California, 11-35. Scrapped after 1946.

MINARETS AND WESTERN RAILWAY COMPANY

(Standard Gauge Captive Railroad of SPL, 1923–1933)

No. 101	**2-8-2**	**48**	**20 x 28**	**174,000**	**180**	**35,700**	**Alco 61858**	**1920**
No. 102	**2-8-2**	**51**	**24½ x 28**	**262,800**	**180**	**50,400**	**Alco 64144**	**1923**
No. 103	**2-8-2**	**51**	**24½ x 28**	**262,800**	**180**	**50,400**	**Alco 64145**	**1923**
No. 104	**2-8-2**	**51**	**24½ x 28**	**262,800**	**180**	**50,400**	**Alco 64146**	**1923**

101. Ex-Portland, Astoria and Pacific, No. 101. Purchased 1922 by M & W. Sold Southern Pacific Railroad 9-32 for $5,000. Sold Aberdeen and Rockfish, No. 40, 1936. Sold Valley Railroad (tourist), Essex, Connecticut, 4-77.
102. Purchased new. Sold Southern Pacific Railroad 1-35. Renumbered SP 3295, 4-35. Scrapped 5-53.
103. Purchased new. Sold Southern Pacific Railroad 1-35. Sold Atlanta and St. Andrews Bay, No. 300. Sold Chicago and Illinois Midland, No. 527. Scrapped 1954.
104. Purchased new. Sold Southern Pacific Railroad 1-35. Renumbered SP 3296, 4-35. Sold Long-Bell Lumber Company, No. 3296, 12-40. Scrapped 3-57.

S.L.R.R.

A Sampling of Shays

Locomotive No. 2 **(above, left)** and No. 1 **(above, right)** of the Sanger Lumber Company stand with their crews on the unloading trestle at Hume Lake on June 30, 1911.

Fresno Flume and Lumber Company's No. 1 **(left)** crosses a low trestle somewhere near Shaver Lake.

George Hume, Sanger Lumber Company president, walks beside Shay No. 3 **(right).** This is the only known photograph of this locomotive.

Madera Sugar Pine Shay No. 3, the *E.M. Fowler,* was one of five Shays used on the company's logging railroad.

The 1-spot Shay of the Yosemite Lumber Company carries a load of logs toward the top of the first big incline in 1914. This photograph was taken at Camp 3 on the south side of the Merced River.

Madera Sugar Pine's No. 2, the *Arthur Hill,* was one of three locomotives named after directors of the company.

Sanger Lumber's No. 1 is shown **(above)** at the Hume Lake engine house in 1914. The locomotive has recently been rebuilt to standard gauge and equipped with air brakes, automatic couplers, and a new stack.

Three-truck Shay No. 5 (below) of the Yosemite Lumber Company is being worked on by the maintenance crew at the new engine house in 1930. The metal structure, built in 1929, stood about a half mile above the incline.

And Other Engines

Madera Sugar Pine's No. 1, a cog-geared saddle-tanker called *Betsy* **(above),** was the smallest railroad engine used on the six southern Sierra logging operations. Although she bounced along the track like a sore-footed mule, the diminutive 0-4-0 had the distinction of being both the first and the longest-lived logging locomotive in southern Sierra history.

The enormous 2-10-2 saddle-tanker **(left)** of the Sugar Pine Lumber Company was used mainly to haul empty log cars up the 4.5 percent grade between Bass Lake and Central Camp. Called the "Minarets" type, the huge engine was the most powerful saddle-tank locomotive ever built.

The Minarets and Western Railroad was a captive operation of the Sugar Pine Lumber Company. It carried logs from Bass Lake to Pinedale using rod locomotives like No. 103 **(left).**

The Plymouth gas-mechanical engine **(above)** of the Madera Sugar Pine Company was used mainly for ballasting and switching.

Trestle No. 14 of the Sugar Pine Lumber Company **(left)** stood 110 feet high. This was one of about 50 trestles built on the company's logging lines.

Log Cars

The six Sierra loggers used a variety of railroad cars over the years. The huge redwood log **(above)** dwarfs the rustic disconnects of the Sanger Lumber Company in 1896. The Madera Sugar Pine Company had link-and-pin couplers on its flat cars **(above, right).** Yosemite Lumber owned no log cars, but the Yosemite Valley Railroad furnished 175 special bulkhead cars **(left)** for use on the steep inclines and in the woods. The Shaver Lake cars **(right)** were company-built models, with outside brake beams and link-and-pin couplers.

184

8972

More Shays in the Sierra

The three views on these two pages give a representative idea of Sierra log trains during railroad days. Three-truck Shay No. 5 **(opposite, top)** of the Yosemite Lumber Company backs through Camp 1 in 1930 on its way to the top of the northside incline about a half-mile distant. The bulkhead log cars all face toward the down side of the incline.

Fresno Flume and Lumber Company Shay No. 1, the *Sierra* **(opposite, bottom)** heads toward Shaver Lake with a load of logs about 1904.

Sanger Lumber Company's first locomotive, the *Sequoia,* looking almost new, crosses a crude log bridge near the lower mill in 1891.

The Toughest Kind of Railroading

Building a Sierra logging railroad involved back-breaking labor. Horse team with scraper **(right)** works in a rock cut near Hume to clear out debris from a blast.

Laborers on the Millwood railroad **(opposite, bottom)** have only hand equipment to help them grade the Sanger Lumber Company's early rail line toward Hoist Ridge in 1892.

Snow was a continuing problem on all the logging operations. The two views **(opposite, top)** along the Yosemite Lumber Company railroad about 1919 are typical examples of sudden Sierra snowstorms.

Getting locomotives to the timber wasn't easy. Shaver Lake Shay No. 1 **(below)** is being hauled piecemeal by 34 horses up the mountain from Fresno to the mill on July 20, 1902.

Passenger Trains

During its last two years of operation, the ill-fated Sugar Pine Lumber Company tried to increase revenues by running excursions to its Central Camp headquarters in the Sierra. Since most of the lumberjacks were then being housed in woods camps some distance away, the five large dormitories and the huge dining hall at Central Camp stood largely unused. In 1930, and twice more in 1931, the company sold "mountain excursions" in conjunction with a Fresno newspaper.

Sightseers were transported over the Minarets and Western Railroad from Pinedale to Central Camp (64 miles) using M&W locomotives and rented Southern Pacific passenger cars. No. 102 **(above)** crosses a trestle at the head end of an excursion train en route to Bass Lake in 1930. At Central Camp, visitors were housed in dormitories and fed in the dining hall. The following day, Sugar Pine log cars, specially fitted with railings and seats **(left),** carried the excursionists 14 miles into the woods to view logging operations. Cost of the package was $1.50.
(U.S. Forest Service Collection, courtesy Craig Konklin)

CHAPTER FOUR

Inclines: The Up-and-Down Railroads

A LOGGING INCLINE was a railroad track, laid to the gauge of the railroad it joined, that carried loaded log cars up or down a grade too steep for a locomotive. Cars were moved along the track—sometimes singly, often several at a time—by means of a sturdy steel cable fastened to the end of the uppermost car. At the top of the grade, a large hoist engine (either steam or electric power) spooled the cable in and out to raise or lower the cars as required.

Inclines were almost exclusively a far-Western device. The unique up-and-down terrain of Pacific Coast timber belts made alternative methods of reaching the trees, such as switchbacks or lengthy contour routes, far more costly and time-consuming to build than going straight up the side of the mountain. Although conditions varied widely with the individual situation, the average incline used only about one-fifth as much track as a comparable series of switchbacks to obtain the same objective. Moreover, inclines could be of lighter construction than ordinary logging railroads because they were not subjected to the tractive effort of heavy locomotives.

Logging historian Kramer Adams called inclines "the peculiar mark of the Western railroad logger; his pride and his glory." Exactly how many were built over the years is not really known, but they must have numbered in the hundreds. During the season of 1926, for example, the *Timberman* magazine reported 50 inclines currently operating in the West, with more planned for the following year. Legend has it that one Western logger without an incline felt so ashamed that he hunted up a mountain and put an incline on it to regain his self-respect.

The first logging incline seems to have been built along the Cosumnes River in the Sierra foothills in 1852. Using a rope-and-pulley arrangement, it lowered log cars a thousand feet down a 45-degree descent. The invention of the steam donkey in 1881 and the development of wire rope a few years later made powered inclines practical. By the turn of the century, large hoist engines were spooling enough cable to haul cars over routes more than a mile and a half in length—sometimes pulling them up grades that exceeded 70 percent. (The grade of a railroad track is the rate of ascent or descent, with a level track rated at zero. One with a rise of three feet in 100 feet, for example, would have a three-percent grade, 10 feet in 100 feet a 10-percent grade, and so on. Although the 45-degree angle of a 100-percent rise was a practical impossibility, some inclines came surprisingly close to reaching it.)

Two types of incline systems predominated: single-cable and counterbalanced. Less popular were the Sessom's system and the Dudley (or Dudler) device. The Sessom's system utilized a special block car coupled ahead of the load. The cable passed from the hoist through the block on the car and back to a tail hold at the top of the incline. The system cut the pull on the line in half but doubled the amount of cable required. The Dudley was a sort of walking donkey mounted on railroad trucks and powered by either a steam or gasoline engine. It moved itself along the incline, dragging logs over the ties behind it or sometimes hauling them on cars, by means of a cable wound several times around a bull drum on the machine. The cable itself was stationary; the ends were attached to trees or stumps at the upper and lower incline terminals.

In a single-cable system, a one-drum hoisting or lowering engine, placed near the head of the incline, dropped loaded cars down or pulled them up depending on the location of the logging railroad connection. Sometimes the incline hoist was installed on the summit of a ridge, where it first pulled cars up one side to the top and then lowered them down the opposite slope to the railroad. Not infrequently, cars were carried over more than one divide, incline following incline, by applying two or more hoists in tandem. The single-cable system found its widest use, however, on temporary inclines where access to a particular pocket of timber above or below the logging railroad was desired.

A counterbalanced incline also employed only a single cable. Instead of spooling it in and out on a drum, however, the counterbalanced system used the weight of a loaded log car, descending on one end of the cable, to pull up an empty log car ascending at the opposite end. The hoist engine acted mainly as a braking device. Several wraps of the cable around the main drum provided all the friction necessary to control the movement of the cars. The arrangement required double tracks where the cars met each other midway on the grade, as well as a series of sheaves and hold-downs to keep the cable in proper alignment. Some counterbalanced inclines were double-tracked from top to bottom; others had a single track from the base to about the midpoint where passing tracks and switches were installed. From here either single or double tracks continued on to the summit. Although counterbalanced inclines doubled the operating speed of similar single-cable setups, their higher construction cost generally restricted their use to substantial, semi-permanent installations.

The six southern Sierra railroad loggers built a total of 20 inclines between 1893 and 1931. The Madera Sugar Pine Company had six, the Sanger Lumber Company seven, the Yosemite Lumber Company four, and the Sugar Pine Lumber Company two (SPL completed a third incline in 1931 but shut down before it could be used). The Fresno Flume and Lumber Company and the Pine Ridge Lumber Company, both primarily early chute-logging shows, built no inclines. Fifteen of the 20 southern Sierra inclines were transitory, single-cable systems designed to reach isolated forest tracts along the logging railroads. When considerable timber was involved, railroad spurs were sometimes built from the end of the incline into the surrounding woods. One or more locomotives were then employed to bring log cars to the hoist. More often, however, some type of heavy yarding equipment was set up at the incline terminus to haul in logs for loading on cars.

The five other inclines consisted of the great steam hoist of the Kings River Lumber Company (Sanger), built atop Hoist Ridge near Sequoia National Park in 1893 to pull cars loaded with giant redwood logs (later rough-cut lumber) out of Converse Basin to a 6,700-foot summit, and then lower them down the opposite side to the railhead; and the four counterbalanced inclines operated by the Yosemite Lumber Company.

Two of the Yosemite inclines were among the most unusual engineering accomplishments in Western steam-logging history. Finished in 1912 and 1924 respectively, they dropped breathtakingly down the nearly vertical slopes on either side of the Merced River Canyon, just west of Yosemite National Park, from timbered crests more than 3,000 feet above. The earlier, southside incline, which contained a vertiginous stretch of 78-percent grade at its upper end, is generally recognized as the steepest logging incline ever built in the world.

The Yosemite Sugar Pine Lumber Company, last of the southern Sierra railroad loggers, shut down its inclines at the close of the 1942 season, and by the end of the decade not a single working incline remained in the United States. Their time, like that of the railroads they served, had come and gone. But they were marvels of ingenuity and invention while they lasted—spectacular performers in the railroad logging show of the West.

The Steepest Incline in the World

Measured on the slope of the track, the original southside incline of the Yosemite Lumber Company ran 8,100 feet from El Portal to the end of Henness Ridge, 3,100 feet above. The 1913 photograph **(facing page)** shows Frank McFadden, first incline foreman, standing on the trestle that spanned the Merced River at the bottom of the slope, very near the junction with the Yosemite Valley Railroad. The incline started up the mountain on a 48-percent grade, changed to a 52-percent grade for several hundred feet, and then dropped to a 45-percent grade until the midpoint was reached. A manual switch was situated just below the midpoint, and the remainder of the route was double-tracked to the top. The last 2,500 feet to the summit reached a grade of 78 percent—the steepest ever known on a logging incline.

The cable, made of 6 x 19 plow steel wire, was 8,600 feet long and 1½ inches in diameter. It was held in position by two overhead holddowns and a series of cast steel sheaves in the center of the tracks on the humps of the grade. Four trestles spanned ravines along the right-of-way. The steam-powered hoist engine at the top weighed 150 tons and had a line speed of 1,300 feet per minute. The counterbalanced system raised an empty car on one end of the cable while lowering a loaded car on the other. Four wraps of the cable around the hoist drum provided all the friction necessary to control the operation. A car could be hooked on and lowered from top to bottom in about eight minutes.

The bulkhead log cars had steel underframes, special center plates, and long side bearings—all designed to handle the 12 tons of extra thrust engendered by the precipitous slope. The incline operated from 1912 through the season of 1923. When the logging show moved to the north side of the Merced River in 1924, the hoist machinery was electrified and used on Incline Number Two, about a mile beyond the second big incline at Trumbull Peak.

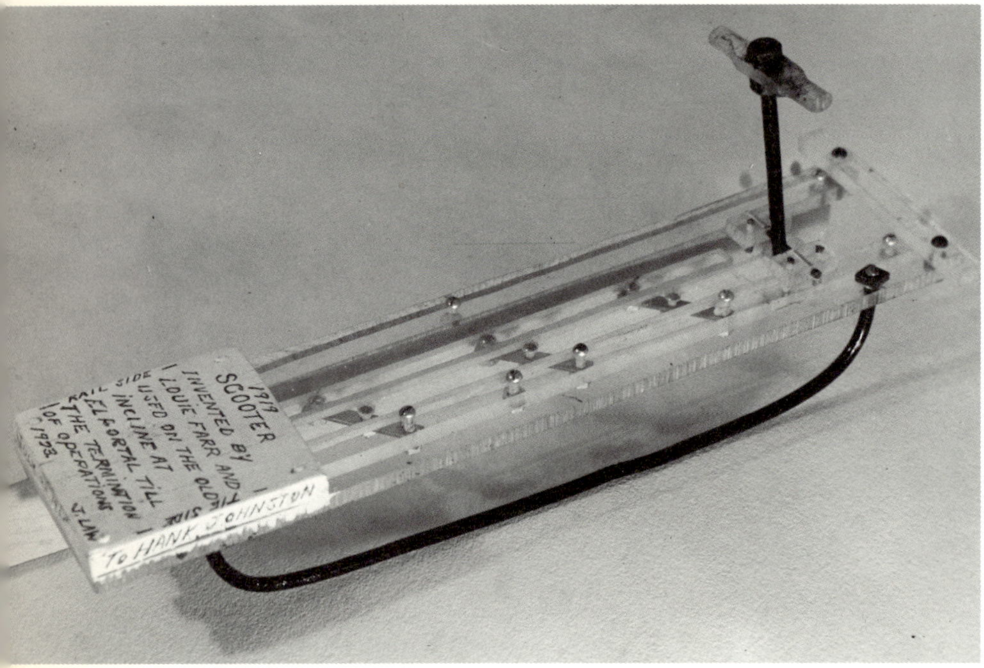

The Toughest Sledding in the World

The photograph (above) shows a plexiglass model built by Jim Law, former Yosemite Lumber Company incline superintendent, of a sled that was used for some years on the southside incline above El Portal. The prototype was built by Louie Farr, a company carpenter, as a means of riding the railroad track down the incline. Made of 2 by 12 lumber, the sled was about six feet long and a foot wide. The left edge of the sled had two cleats, which straddled one rail, fastened to the underside. The right edge had a curved metal bar on the bottom that rode on top of the ties at rail height, thus keeping the conveyance level. Ties that were slightly higher than normal were trimmed out with an adz to accommodate the bar. Pulling back on the handle in front tightened the cleats against the rail, which provided the rider with a crude sort of friction brake. Jim Law recalls many instances of loggers riding the sled down the steep 8,100-foot slope over the years. The record from top to bottom was two and a half minutes—a speed in excess of 35 miles an hour! Eventually, however, so many loggers were injured when the sled jumped the track at high speeds that the use of the unique vehicle was discontinued.

Building the great southside incline of the Yosemite Lumber Company in 1911-12 was a remarkable engineering feat. The fourth steam donkey up the hill is seen **(right)** as it ponderously pulls itself across one of the four trestles on the right-of-way in 1912.

The various dips in the El Portal incline are clearly evident in this early photograph **(left).** A tank car carrying fuel oil is beginning its ascent near the bottom of the grade.

At the Hoist

The head of the incline (Camp 1) on Henness Ridge **(above)** served as the southside logging headquarters of the Yosemite Lumber Company for a dozen years. The big steam hoist is housed in the sheet-metal building with the tall smokestack. The incline cable runs from the hoist drum in the building, through the two holddowns along the tracks, and eventually to the top of the incline itself, which lies about 50 yards beyond the area shown in the front edge of the picture. Empty cars were taken out on the left-hand track; loaded cars brought in on the right-hand track.

Second Incline

The second great Yosemite incline **(facing page)** lay about five miles west of the original incline, just across from present Indian Flat. Although not as steep as the first one, the northside slope reached a maximum grade of 68 percent along its 8,300-foot length. More than 400 rollers and three overhead holddowns were required to maintain the 1½-inch wire rope in proper position because of a curve at the top with a 500-foot radius. A second curve of lesser radius at the bottom enabled the incline tracks to merge with the Yosemite Valley Railroad main line at the station of Incline. The incline hoist, electrically powered by two Westinghouse 200-horsepower motors, weighed 320,000 pounds. As with the first incline, the right-of-way was double-tracked from the top to just below the midpoint, and single-tracked from there to the bottom.

Jimmy Mullen, longtime lookout for the company, rides the front of a log car **(right)** as it rounds the curve at the top of the incline. Mullen is undoubtedly en route to his position in the lookout shanty nearby. Lookouts were stationed at the top and bottom of the incline, with direct telephone connections to the hoist engineer.

Some of the cable-guide rollers adjoining the curve at the bottom of the second big incline are visible in this photograph **(left).**

A loaded log car is being readied to go down the mountain **(below)** from the head of the second big incline near the top of Trumbull Peak. The hoist house can be seen at the top left; the railroad main line to the woods curves to the right around the side of the mountain.

The Yosemite Lumber Company constructed a smaller counterbalanced incline about a mile beyond Trumbull Peak in 1924 to reach timber stands to the northeast. The 1,600-foot incline, known as Incline Number Two **(right)**, had a maximum grade of 45 percent and was double-tracked from top to bottom. The old steam hoist from the southside incline (converted to electricity) supplied the head-end power.

Fuel for the locomotives working the woods above Incline Number Two was transported by tank cars brought up over the Yosemite Valley Railroad. The tank cars then had to be pulled up both inclines in order to reach the logging area. The photograph **(above)** shows a tank car that derailed about halfway up Incline Number Two in 1925. Over the years, however, there were very few wrecks on the various Yosemite inclines, which was remarkable in view of the hazards involved.

YV

Camp 20 Incline

The fourth Yosemite incline was situated along the logging railroad about 15 miles north of Trumbull Peak. Built in 1938, the incline was a double-tracked, counterbalanced affair similar to Incline Number Two with one notable exception. In this operation, loaded log cars were pulled *up* the 1,200-foot-long slope. The three pictures show: **(facing page)** a car beginning the ascent up the incline's 30-percent grade; **(above)** the top of the incline where a huge 14 x 16 Willamette steam yarder furnished the necessary hoisting power; and **(right)** a log car nearing the top of the grade. (All Jim Law Collection)

Sugar Pine Hoists

The Sugar Pine Lumber Company operated two inclines along its logging railroad south of Central Camp between 1928 and 1931.

The Brown's Creek incline **(left)** ran off the railroad's 9 line down a 40-percent grade to Camp 6, where spur tracks branched out into the surrounding woods. About 3,500 feet long, it was used to pull logs up to the main-line railroad for two seasons.

In 1930 the company built this 4,500-foot incline **(facing page)** to carry log cars up a 33-percent grade from its logging show near Benedict Meadow.

Both inclines were powered by a unique 750-horsepower electric hoist **(below),** specially built by the Willamette Iron and Steel Company for the purpose. Mounted on a railcar chassis, the hoist was portable and could be pulled to any point along the logging railroad.

Converse Basin

The first Converse Basin mill of the Sanger Lumber Company began cutting on June 30, 1897. The mill burned down on November 11, 1905, and was rebuilt in slightly different form in the spring of 1906. The second mill **(right)** was a two-band structure with a daily capacity of 175,000 board feet. The incline to the top of Hoist Ridge ran for almost a mile from the left of the mill to the summit. Loggers **(below)** walk the lower part of the incline to their camp, partway up the slope, after finishing a shift.

The Great Converse Hoist

The incline hoist built atop Hoist Ridge by the Sanger Lumber Company in the mid-1890s pulled railroad cars loaded with lumber (usually three cars at a time) from the Converse Basin mill to the 6,700-foot summit. Here the cable was transferred to the opposite end of the three-car convoy, and the load was then lowered down a half-mile incline on the Millwood side of Hoist Ridge to the railhead. When nine cars had been assembled at the bottom, a Shay locomotive pulled the train to Millwood, at which point the boards were sent down the flume to the finishing mill at Sanger. The photograph **(facing page)** of the Millwood side of Hoist Ridge shows a single car, carrying both lumber and passengers, descending the incline at the end of the cable.

The interior of the hoist house on Hoist Ridge is shown **(below)** in 1896. A contemporary account of the hoisting machinery described it as follows: "The hoist consists of two J.B. Jardine boilers operating a 350-horsepower Lidgerwood double-cylindered reversible engine with 18 x 36 inch cylinders. The 18-inch pinion on the shaft is geared to an 18-foot spur wheel on a 15-foot drum, which is 18 feet long. On this works the cable, 1-1/8 inches thick, 1½ miles long, and weighing 17,000 pounds. An automatic screw device places the cable in proper position on the drum. A smaller drum, with a lesser cable, is used to pull cars over the level to either side of the incline, so the big cable can then be hooked on to lower its load in either direction as required."

A temporary single-track incline ran northwest from the Hoist Ridge summit of the Sanger Lumber Company's Converse Basin operation to a pocket of timber in a hole known as Camp 6. Here logs were brought by chute to the foot of the incline **(above),** loaded on railroad cars, and then pulled by a donkey yarder up a steep slope to a junction with the incline tracks on Hoist Ridge. The big hoist was then used to lower the cars to the mill in Converse Basin to be cut into lumber. Some large redwood logs **(opposite, right)** were taken out of the area, one car at a time, by means of this incline.

Next two pages: A similar situation existed at the Sanger Lumber Company's Hume Lake mill. This 1915 photograph shows log cars being loaded at the foot of a steep incline east of Hume Lake. The cars will be hauled by cable and steam donkey up to the railroad main line.

CHAPTER FIVE

The Great Lumber Flumes

THE V-FLUME was undoubtedly the most unconventional form of lumber transport ever conceived. Imagine a slim wooden water trough—literally a man-made river—twisting its circuitous way through the forest and down the mountains, here clinging precariously to sheer canyon walls, there bridging gorges on trestles sometimes a hundred feet or more in the air, all the while carrying bundles of rough-cut lumber 40, 50, or even 60 miles from mountain mill to trunkline railroad in the flatlands below.

Credit for the first successful lumber flume is generally given to one J.W. Haines, who built a 12-mile, V-shaped trough down the east side of the Sierra to the Carson Valley and the Comstock Lode in Nevada in 1859. Unlike conventional box-shaped flumes, which had been used for various types of water transport since pioneer times but in which boards tended to wedge against the sides, Haines' V-flume was almost self-clearing; if a jam started, the backhead lifted the planks into the widening top of the flume. Moreover, the V-flume took less lumber to construct and less water to operate than the old box-type affair.

California lumbermen soon copied Haines' innovative transportation method. A half-dozen V-flumes were constructed in the northern Sierra in the 1870s and '80s (one nearly 40 miles in length), but none achieved any particular success.

In the southern Sierra, however, the development of the V-flume marked the beginning of a whole new era in mountain logging. By locating the sawmill itself in the timber and shipping only usable lumber out of the mountains, the age-old problem of exorbitant transportation costs was finally overcome. As a result, between 1874 and 1894 the three longest lumber flumes in the world were built down the slopes of the western Sierra to the San Joaquin Valley within a few miles of each other. The California Lumber Company completed its 52-mile flume to Madera in 1876; the Kings River Lumber Company built a 54-mile flume from Millwood to Sanger in 1889–90; and the Fresno Flume and Irrigation Company constructed its 45-mile flume to Clovis from Shaver Lake in 1893–94. (The Madera flume was rebuilt to Sugar Pine in 1899–1900, a distance of 54 miles overall, and the upper portion of the Sanger flume was rerouted to the new sawmill at Hume Lake in 1909, making it 59 miles in length—the longest lumber flume ever known.)

During the 56 years between 1876 and 1931, the last season of fluming in the Sierra, at least one of the great V-flumes operated every summer. For 19 of those years, all three flumes were in use, and in eight other years, two flumes shipped lumber down the mountains.

V-flumes generally consisted of two flat sides made up of boards 1¼ to 1½ inches thick, which were nailed together to form a right angle. The sides varied from 32 inches to 48 inches in width, depending on the individual application. The boards were assembled in 16-foot sections called "boxes," and braced securely on cross sills and caps atop a continuous series of trestles of varying heights.

The desired grade was one inch of fall per box, or 27 feet to the mile, but a constant gradient was impossible to maintain despite the use of trestles more than a hundred feet high in places. On the upper Sanger flume below Millwood, for example, the flume dropped down a 23-percent grade for about a thousand yards, or 1,200 feet to the mile, and the average fall over the first 13 miles of the route was a precipitous 330 feet to the mile. Conversely, in the nearly level San Joaquin Valley near the flume terminus, the water flowed barely fast enough to keep the lumber moving.

Construction costs of the three Sierra flumes averaged about $6,000 a mile, or a little over a dollar a running foot—this at a time when the buying power of a dollar was more than 10 times the current rate. Although far cheaper to build than a comparable railroad, flumes required constant maintenance. Repair crews normally worked all winter to ready each flume for the following season, sometimes using more than a million board feet of lumber in the

Bundles of lumber float down the Madera flume on their way to the finishing mill, a distance of 54 miles. (U.S. Forest Service Collection)

process.

Lumber was tossed into the flumes at the mountain sawmills in bundles from 10 to 13 inches thick, bound together at each end by pointed iron clamps and wooden wedges. As the bundles progressed down the flume, they were tied together with short ropes into increasingly longer trains (to prevent jackknifing) by flume "herders" stationed every few miles along the route. The herders, living in isolated shacks at strategic spots, ran along narrow catwalks watching for jam-ups or leaks on their section. At night, or in rainy or icy weather, the six- to eight-inch catwalks were precarious walkways at best, and more than one herder met his end over the side of a high trestle.

In addition to transporting lumber, flumes also carried passengers and supplies to points along the line. Homemade wooden boats about 16 feet long and shaped roughly in the form of a "W" with a flat board on top were used for this purpose. Some people rode flume boats for thrills—and there were plenty of those on the steep sections—others because an injury or other emergency required speedy transportation out of the mountains. On several occasions, dead bodies were even lashed to boats and floated down to the coroner in the San Joaquin Valley.

Mrs. J.C. Forkner, whose father L.P. Swift was one of the principals in the Fresno Flume and Irrigation Company, recalls her father organizing flume party rides with six or eight persons on a boat when the Clovis flume was new. The group rode about 15 miles to the Saddle, where they got off and returned to Shaver Lake by team and wagon. Later, after the flume became somewhat battered from lumber shipments, it was not considered safe for riding except in an emergency.

The three great lumber flumes played a unique role in the steam-logging era of the southern Sierra. Billions of board feet of lumber were floated swiftly and economically down their slender waterways over the years, and without them there would have been no mountain sawmills.

Flumes used no energy, created no pollution, and delivered water for irrigation as a by-product. Would that a modern diesel logging truck could make that statement!

The ensuing photographs are a representative sampling of the flumes in their heyday—the way it was in the Sierra, once upon a time.

Daredevil construction workers pose for the camera during the building of a long trestle on the Madera flume in 1899.

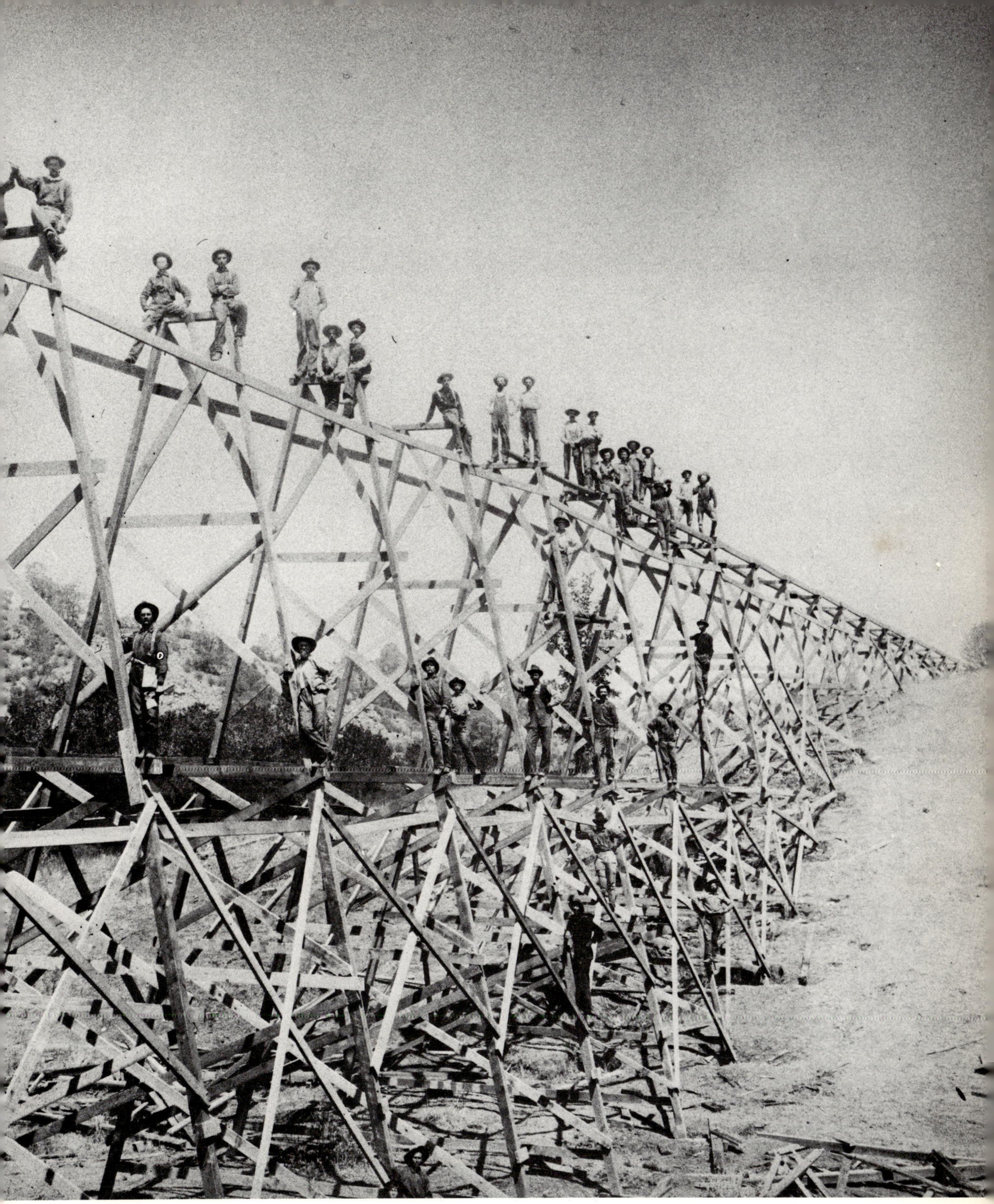

Flumes

Although the three big flumes were similar in construction, each had certain unique features. The picture **(opposite, top left)** shows the highest trestle on the Shaver Lake flume, more than 90 feet above the bed of Musick Creek. Note the double construction, with the V-flume on top and the box-flume framework underneath. The same design is evident in another view of the Shaver flume **(right)** as it passes through "Devil's Canyon," about a half mile below the Shaver mill. Use of the box flume was discontinued soon after the flume was built because of lawsuits by other claimants to the water rights.

Repair work on the Madera flume was a continuing thing for three decades. These flume workers seem to be showing off a bit **(opposite, top right)**. Another flume repairman **(opposite, bottom)** poses in a more conventional manner.

Flume Herders

Two youthful flume herders take a break at an auxiliary loading station on the Sanger flume just below Hume Lake **(left).** The flume herder on the Shaver Lake flume **(opposite, top)** uses his pickaroon to straighten out a jam near Pine Ridge. The two views of flume houses were taken along the Madera flume **(bottom, left)** and the Shaver Lake flume **(opposite, bottom).** A flume boat, laden with supplies **(below),** floats across a trestle somewhere on the Madera Sugar Pine Lumber Company flume about 1902.

This is the head of the Sanger Lumber Company flume at Millwood in the 1890s. Railroad tracks and water tank are visible above the lumber-loading area. (Harold Schutt Collection)

Lumber Flumes

The flume frog (left) at Sugar Pine joined various branches of the flume into one unit for the trip to Madera. Bundles of clamped lumber at Millwood **(below)** and Sugar Pine **(opposite, top)** are being tossed into the flumes by loaders. The unusual truck pictured at Sugar Pine in 1924 **(opposite, bottom)** was used to carry boards from the mill to the flume head.

#43
S.72

High trestles of various construction were required in many places along the flumes to keep the grades reasonably even. Compare the long trestle on the Sanger flume **(opposite, top left)** with the two views of the Shaver Lake flume **(opposite, top right)** and **(opposite, bottom).**

Flume boats were used on all three flumes to transport supplies. They also provided quick transportation from one point to another. An early flume rider **(below)** negotiates the Shaver Lake flume near Pine Ridge. His hat marks him as a U.S. Forest Service employee.

Flume Terminals

At the Madera drying yards, an electric-powered ''flume cart'' **(right)** raised boards to the tops of the drying piles by means of a pulley arrangement. (U.S. Forest Service Collection)

A bundle of lumber pops out of the flume **(bottom)** onto a conveyor belt at the Madera flume terminus.

The striking similarity between the Shaver Lake flume terminal at Clovis **(opposite, top)** and the Sanger Lumber Company terminal at Sanger **(opposite, bottom)** is readily apparent in these two excellent early photographs.

CHAPTER SIX

From Ox Carts to Skylines

THE PROCEDURES for getting timber from woods to mill underwent considerable change during the steam-logging era of the southern Sierra. In the early years of the Madera Flume and Trading Company, logging was accomplished in rudimentary fashion. Trees were felled and bucked into logs 12 to 20 feet long; the logs were then rolled onto crude wooden wagons and toilsomely hauled to the mill by ox teams. The bulky log carts, put together in the company's own blacksmith shop, consisted of four wooden wheels with a heavy bolster mounted between each pair, a coupling pole extending from the rear pair to the front pair, and a stiff tongue projecting out the front for guiding and hitching. The wheels, sliced from foot sections of a tree, usually had hoops of iron or steel for tires.

By the time the Kings River Lumber Company and the Fresno Flume and Irrigation Company began cutting in the early 1890s, log chutes had largely replaced ox carts in the woods. Chutes were essentially a continuous line of two parallel poles placed end to end and connected by a series of lap joints. Cut from young trees 20 to 60 feet long with a minimum of taper, the poles had their inner sides hewn smooth with a broadax to form a trough six to 18 inches wide depending on the size of the timber being logged. Where the topography permitted, chutes were embedded directly in the ground and required little external bracing or support. On steep pitches and in crossing depressions, chute poles were mounted on built-up crib work or securely anchored trestles, as rigidity was all important.

Horses, mules, and even oxen were employed at first to drag logs along chutes from cutting area to landing. By 1900, however, steam donkeys had virtually eliminated the use of animals in the Sierra forests. The sturdy little machines did not get tired and required no feed and little care. Moreover, they skidded logs in half an hour that took animal power half a day to move. As time went on, larger multi-drum steam donkeys made possible the use of extensive main-line chutes, sometimes a mile or more in length, which were fed by a network of smaller chutes, each with its own yarding engine at points along the way.

Five of the six southern Sierra railroad loggers utilized chutes extensively prior to 1915 (the Sugar Pine Lumber Company did not begin cutting until 1923). Pine Ridge Lumber, Fresno Flume and Lumber, and Sanger Lumber, in fact, were almost exclusively ground-lead logging shows during their lifetimes.

High-lead logging came into general use in the Sierra during World War I, after being introduced in California in 1913. In this system, a spar tree 100 feet or more in height was set up near the railroad landing. The main 1½-inch yarding cable was then passed from the drum of a big steam donkey nearby through a block hung at the top of the spar pole and out to a tail block anchored at the far end of the run. Logs were fastened to this main line by a choke-cable noose around the front end and dragged to the landing, often from as far as 2,000 feet away. As the main-line cable was reeled in, a lighter haul-back line, following the general ground level, was fed out to the tail block and could then be used to pull the big main line back to the cutting area for the operation to begin anew.

In a high-lead setup, unlike earlier ground yarding, the front ends of the logs were elevated, which largely prevented their getting hung up on stumps, rocks, or depressions. In addition, a higher skidding speed was possible as soon as the log reached the point near enough to the spar tree to have the cable exert a lifting tendency—usually about 500 feet away, depending on the terrain.

Where deep ravines or sharp slopes prevailed, skyline cable systems proved highly proficient. A skyline show consisted of a tail tree at the high-lead setting, and a head tree and yarder at the railroad landing. Running between the head and tail trees was a heavy fixed cable, suspended high in the air

These three Madera Sugar Pine lumberjacks wear the customary attire of the early Sierra logger. Note the calked boots (called "corks" by everyone), stagged-off pants, suspenders, felt hats, and long johns. Never washed, the pants were worn until they became so stiff with pitch they were unusable. (U.S. Forest Service Collection)

This early photograph shows a typical ox team and wooden-wheeled wagon at Pine Ridge during the days of animal logging.

from jacks hung near the top of each spar. The cable supported a movable carriage that rode along the skyline on two sheaves. Logs were yarded to the high-lead spar in normal fashion, then tied to the skyline cable rigging with chokers, usually several at a time. At a given signal, the donkey puncher at the head-tree yarder began to reel in the main line. This lifted the log load high off the ground, then pulled the carriage and its dangling cargo along the skyline to the head-tree landing at the railroad.

From about 1918 on, the Madera Sugar Pine Company and the Yosemite Lumber Company adopted the innovative overhead techniques at most of their railroad landings with considerable success. The premier exponent of the new systems, however, was the short-lived Sugar Pine Lumber Company, one of the very few logging operations ever to use all-electric equipment in the woods. The company yarded with a variety of powerful electric skidders and loaders during its nine-year run, and its abrupt financial demise was in no way caused by any shortcomings in its woods machinery.

Much of the logging in the southern Sierra, especially during the earliest years of the steam era, was extremely wasteful and destructive. No care was given to saving young timber, and clear-cutting left no seed trees standing for reproduction. In the mid-1920s both Madera Sugar Pine and Sugar Pine Lumber began cutting on Forest Service lands under federal regulations. Down came the height of the high-lead block from 100 feet or more to a maximum of 35 feet, so logs would not stray all over the landscape when being yarded. Rangers selectively marked all trees to be cut, and young growth was protected from damage. Brush and slash had to be piled for burning the following winter by special clean-up crews.

Most lumberjacks resented the government rules at first, considering them a real handicap to production, but as time went on and the benefits became clearly evident, opposition to the restrictions ceased. Under the new rules, it was hard to tell that logging had occurred at all after two or three years had passed.

Today, 60 years after the glory days of Sierra lumbering, skylines and high leads are still widely prevalent in the big timber of the Pacific Northwest despite the introduction of helicopters, balloons, and other modern logging systems. Factory-rigged portable steel poles have replaced the old spar tree on big operations, and skyline carriages are often radio controlled, but the basic techniques remain the same. Skyline logging, in fact, is on the increase in recent years because it creates less environmental damage than almost any other method of transporting logs from the woods.

Overhead logging disappeared from the southern Sierra a long time ago. For a good many years now, almost all commercial logging has been accomplished with diesel tractors, portable loaders, and trucks under strict government supervision. The shameful "cut-out-and-get-out" practices of bygone times have been replaced by reason in the handling of our forests.

Bull Whackers

Handling oxen in the woods was an art in itself. The ox teams were driven by bull whackers whose profanity, according to legend, could steam the bark off a tree. These two views, taken near Millwood during the first days of the Sanger Lumber Company operation, show **(right)** animals being readied to move down a dirt skid road, and **(below)** a team of oxen working a chute-logging show in the Sierra redwoods. The giant log has been bucked and is in the process of being blasted into sections that the oxen can handle. (Both Harold Schutt Collection)

The Fallers

Sierra fallers were artists with their double-bitted axes. The undercuts in the great trees looked almost as smooth as if they had been sawed. Once the undercut was completed, fallers drew a long cross-cut saw back and forth across the trunk from the opposite side until the tree finally toppled over in the direction of the undercut. Faller **(left)** begins an undercut in a big Sugar Pine near Shaver Lake about 1896. European fallers **(below)** stand beside their handiwork at Madera Sugar Pine. The most challenging task of all, however, was presented by the giant Sierra redwoods logged by the Sanger Lumber Company at Converse Basin **(facing page).** It sometimes took two men a week or more to hack out an undercut in these big trees. (Harold Schutt Collection)

Logging the Sierra Redwoods

Lumberjacks at Converse Basin pose for the photographer **(above)** on a summer Sunday about 1900. The huge undercut has been completed, and the long cross-cut saw will be put to use the following day to bring down the giant redwood. The saws, which sometimes exceeded 25 feet, were made by brazing two regular saws together. (Harold Schutt Collection)

Big Bill Mills, who stood well over six feet and weighed more than 230 pounds, has just jumped up on the quivering stump of a 25-foot redwood as the severed giant hurtles toward the ground **(facing page).** Mills was strong as an ox and had a hand in falling more of the big trees than any other person. He liked to show off his skill and daring with stunts like this.

Handling the great trees once they were on the ground was not easy. Logs too big to be moved by chute were blasted apart using black powder dropped into auger holes. In the Converse Basin scene **(above),** buckers stand on springboards to saw the trunk into logs. The men on top of the bole are preparing to use augers to drill holes, into which they will drop powder charges. Sometimes the logs split apart evenly **(left),** but at other times the wood simply shattered into useless pieces.

Facing page: A trail of logs is being assembled on a logging chute at Converse Basin. Huge trails were pulled to the mill from a mile or more away by big bull donkeys. (Harold Schutt Collection)

510

Log Chutes

The southern Sierra loggers made extensive use of chutes, even after the advent of newer techniques. The long cribwork chute **(right)** was part of the vast network of chutes constructed by the Sanger Lumber Company at Converse Basin. Millions of board feet of lumber were required for the miles of chutes in the basin. (Harold Schutt Collection)

Madera Sugar Pine built a series of chutes to log the Fresno Dome area in 1924. The logger **(below)** prepares to transfer the cable at the top of a steep grade to the other side of the block, so the log can be pulled to the landing **(opposite, bottom).**

In the Woods

Long augers hang from the top of a huge Sierra redwood log **(above)** as the crew poses for a photographer in Converse Basin about 1900. Logs this large had to be blasted apart before they could be moved to the chute. (Harold Schutt Collection)

The Fresno flume and Lumber Company used miles of chutes to bring logs to Shaver Lake before the logging railroad was built in 1902. A long trail of logs **(opposite, top)** passes along a trestle adjoining a woods camp a few miles above Shaver Lake.

Head of a chute at Madera Sugar Pine is shown **(opposite, bottom).** A log trail has just arrived, ready to be rolled down a landing to the railroad, which is out of sight to the right.

Big wheels were used briefly at Hume Lake to drag logs in from the woods with horses **(above).** The wheels were first rolled over a downed log, and the front end of the log then attached to the tongue and lifted off the ground. In general, however, the Sierra terrain was too steep for this method.

Steam bucking saws were often employed at chute heads to cut long logs into more convenient lengths. The scene **(below)** shows a steam saw at work on the Yosemite Lumber operation above El Portal in 1915. The young logger **(right)** drives in an anchor to hold the steam saw to the log at a Madera Sugar Pine chute head. Steam power comes from the donkey engine in the rear. (U.S. Forest Service Collection)

Moving a Steam Donkey

Steam donkeys pulled themselves to new positions in the woods once an area had been logged out. Blocks were secured to stumps or trees up ahead, and the main line then threaded through the blocks and back to the yarder. By reeling in the line, the yarder slowly pulled itself forward. The action was repeated until the desired location was reached. In rough country, a donkey was fortunate to move itself a quarter mile in a day. The pictures **(above and below)** show a donkey on the move at the Fresno Flume and Lumber Company logging show above Shaver Lake.

A big yarder of the Yosemite Lumber Company **(facing page)** slowly pulls itself down a slope to a railroad car about 1937. Once it is secured on the car, it will be transported to a new logging area. (Jim Law Collection)

Skylines

Skyline and high-lead logging came into general use in the southern Sierra during World War I. An early skyline **(left)** carries a log to a landing at Madera Sugar Pine about 1915.

The skyline on the northside operations of the Yosemite Lumber Company **(below)** has just dropped a log at the head tree for loading on a railroad car.

The Sugar Pine Lumber Company used several different types of loading and yarding equipment in the woods. The company's "car unit" **(facing page)** was an unusual electric-powered machine. Mounted on a standard railroad car, it could be pulled along the logging spurs behind a locomotive to almost any desired location.

Next two pages: A Yosemite Lumber Company crew performs crotch-line loading along the logging railroad above El Portal about 1916.

ALLEY F.R.

Log Loading

The Sierra railroad loggers used many different loading techniques over the years. In the early days of the Madera Sugar Pine railroad **(above),** gravity roll-ways and hand jacks predominated. At Shaver Lake **(right)** parbuckling (a cable passed under and back over a log causing it to roll when the cable was pulled) was widely employed. In later years steam-powered booms took over. The scenes at Madera Sugar Pine **(opposite, top)** and Sanger Lumber's Hume Lake show **(opposite, bottom)** illustrate two types of power loaders.

LOADING
LOGS

The McGiffert Loader

Madera Sugar Pine and Sanger Lumber both used McGiffert log loaders at various times. The McGiffert supported itself on four corner posts, which straddled the railroad track on the outside of the ties. This permitted empty cars to pass under the deck on the main track. A swing boom on the front lifted logs onto the cars as they passed through. McGifferts are shown at work near Hume Lake **(below)** and in pieces at Madera Sugar Pine **(left).** The McGiffert moved itself by dropping a pair of trucks to the track, which raised the corner posts off the ties. Power was transmitted to the axles by sprocket chains. According to old-timers, the Madera loader frequently derailed while attempting to move itself along the logging railroad.

Dolbeer's Donkey

The Dolbeer steam donkey shown at Shaver Lake **(above)** was the machine that ousted oxen from the skid roads of the West. It got the name "donkey" from a ship's auxiliary engine, because John Dolbeer, its inventor, had been a naval engineer before turning logger. The Dolbeer was a small steam engine that turned a capstan to reel in rope with the power of many oxen. After wire cable replaced manila rope, loggers began to pull in logs from great distances away. Donkey engines soon got bigger, better, and more versatile until they became the standard of the industry. The donkey remained the power of the Sierra forests until the diesel engine did to the donkey what the donkey had done to the bulls.

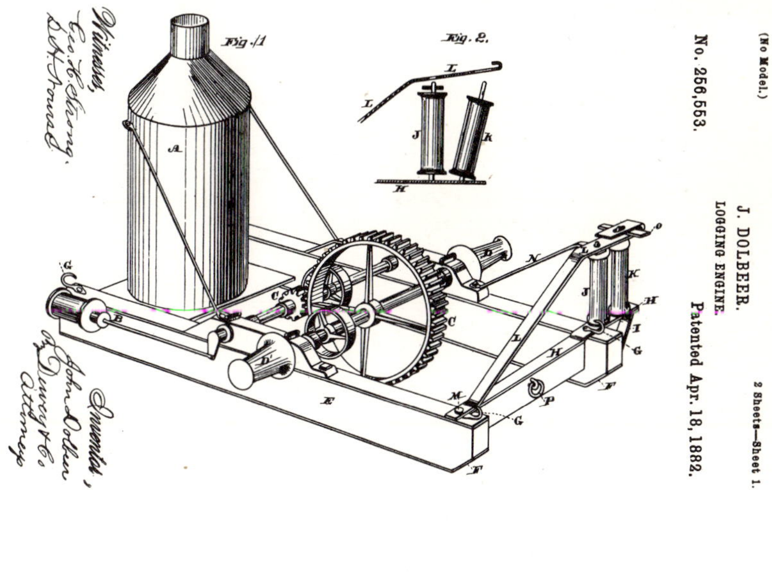

John Dolbeer's original drawing of the donkey engine.

One of John Dolbeer's early products is seen at work in Converse Basin about 1900. Note the coils of cable on the ground. The cable was not held on a drum on the first Dolbeers, but merely turned three or four times around the capstan, and spooled off into a pile as the logs came in. (Harold Schutt Collection)

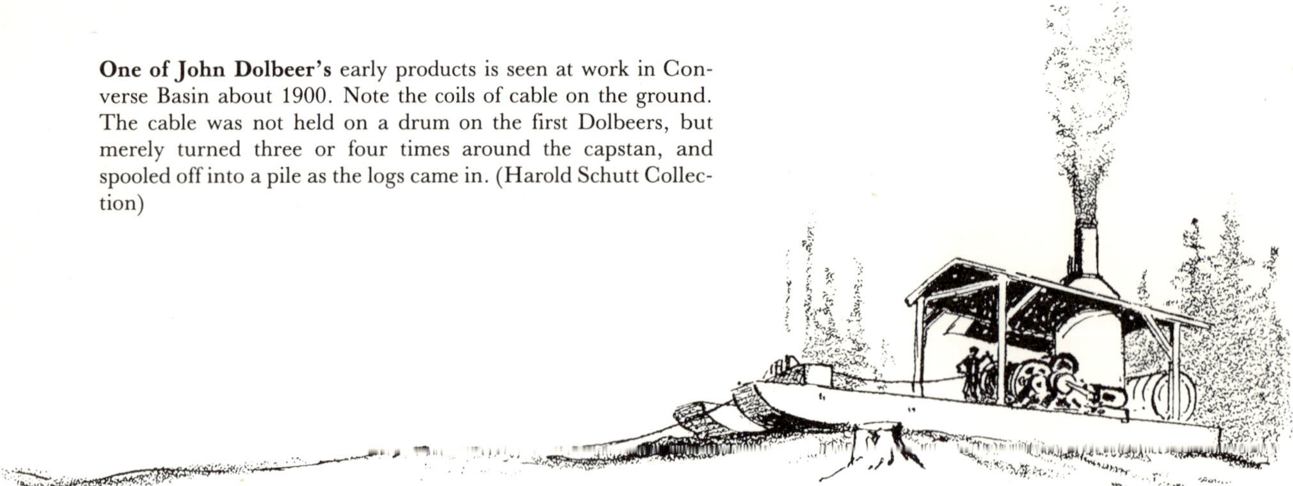

Chute Riders

Keeping the chutes lubricated to prevent excessive friction was the chute-greaser's job. The worker riding the end of the log trail **(right)** at Shaver Lake is applying animal fat to the chute from a pail hanging below him. The chute will now be ready for the next trail to come in.

Big Foot Mike rides a chute boat **(below)** at Yosemite Lumber Company's southside operations in 1915. Chute boats were hollowed-out logs that carried the dogs, chains, and chokers out to the logging area as the back line returned the main cable. Note the bare wires paralleling the chute. The chute rider signaled instructions to the yarding engineer by shorting the wires with a metal-tipped pole as he was pulled along the route.

Railroad Loggers

There was no such thing as a ''typical'' Sierra lumberjack. Loggers came in a wide variety of shapes, sizes, ages, and nationalities, as this early picture **(right),** taken on the Madera Sugar Pine logging show, aptly demonstrates. (U.S. Forest Service Collection)

A big Willamette compound steam yarder works the woods near Sugar Pine **(below).** The yarder is mounted on a timber ''sled''—heavy cross timbers hewed to fit, and bolted together to make a stout frame.

An assemblage of 126 men, women, and children poses on a huge redwood stump near Millwood in 1888. This holiday photograph shows the entire population of an early Sierra logging camp—all gathered on the stump of a single tree! (Harold Schutt Collection)

CHAPTER SEVEN

A Rough and Dangerous Life

ABOUT THE ONLY THING a worker in an early Sierra lumber camp could count on with certainty was backbreaking labor from dawn to dusk, six or seven days a week, for pay of $30 a month and board. Loggers worked hard, played hard when they had the chance, faced death every day, and grew old in their youth—if they lived long enough. There were no unions, no compensation laws, no fringe benefits, no retirement plans, and no recourse to the arbitrary rules of the employer except quitting.

Logging camps were primitive places in the 1870s and '80s, usually nothing more than a motley assortment of crude wooden shacks erected in the woods. A man's bunk was his castle if he could stand the acrid odor of sweat, tobacco, booze, and spittle that pervaded the buildings. One early Sierra lumberjack wrote of his experiences at camp: "I was told to pick out any shack I wanted with an empty bed in it. No spring cots, just a board bunk with from four to six men crammed into a small space. Furnish my own water bucket, wash pan, and everything else. We used cedar boughs for mattresses on account of bedbugs, and I mean BEDBUGS! Lots of body lice too. If you wanted a bath, heat your own water in a coal oil can. Toilets were not hard to find—just follow your nose. Flies till they nearly drove you crazy, most all hatched in the outhouse. No laundry, do your own or not as you pleased. At least half the men got pretty rank before they learned their lesson. More than once we had to tie a man to a chair and water him down with the fire hose before he got the message."

Rugged men in a rugged job, most lumberjacks accepted their rudimentary living conditions as a matter of course, but bad food or short rations were not tolerated. A logger might burn 8,000 calories during a typical 10-hour workday—three times the ordinary man doing an ordinary job—and he needed plenty of nourishment to sustain him. An experienced logger starting a new job often scouted the camp pigpen before looking up the boss. If the hogs were too fat, he knew the men were not eating all the food—a bad sign. On the other hand, lean hogs meant few table scraps, which indicated that the cook knew his business. An incompetent cook could clean out a lumber camp faster than a forest fire.

A cook's helper at a Madera Sugar Pine camp summons the logging crew to dinner by banging on an old circular saw with the back of an ax. (U.S. Forest Service Collection)

Because most labor in the Sierra logging camps was employed for only about seven months a year, it was inclined to be unstable. A Forest Service report of the day explained the situation as follows: "There are two classes of labor—one to which belong most of the men in the skilled and better paid positions. This group winters on the ranches and in the towns of central California, frequently returning to the same operation season after season; the other class is purely transient and works on one job from a few days to a season and then moves on to the next. Mill

Camp 1, near Big Sandy, was a typical portable woods camp used on the Madera Sugar Pine logging railroad.

crews are usually much less transient than the woods force.

"Labor is secured by hiring in the nearest city or large town. In the spring the higher-grade employees make application to the superintendent, some even being hired by letter. Many of the other men do the same, but it is frequently necessary for the logging superintendent to visit the nearest city and engage men, paying their way to the work and guaranteeing their unpaid board bills. Later in the summer, when the men become restless and begin to leave, it is often necessary to secure men through employment agencies, which entails paying the fares to the plant. More and more, the felling, limbing, and bucking jobs are paid by contract—the more the men produce, the more they make."

As time went on, conditions became downright civilized in most Sierra camps. Regular communities grew up around the mountain sawmills at Shaver Lake, Sugar Pine, Millwood, and later, Converse Basin and Hume Lake. Companies built permanent houses for married workers and hotel-type dormitories for single employees. Church services, movies, schools, and professional medical care were provided during the season. The California Workmen's Compensation Act of January 1, 1914, rendered the employer liable for compensation for all personal injuries sustained by employees during the course of their work.

In the woods, portable camps consisting of sturdy wooden cabins, a cookhouse, blacksmith shop, saw-filing shop, stable, and perhaps a commissary, were set up near each logging site. When the area had been logged over, the buildings were loaded on railroad cars by means of donkey engines and moved to a new location.

By far the grandest camp of all was the mountain headquarters of the Sugar Pine Lumber Company. Built in 1922–23 at a cost of more than $600,000, Central Camp, as it was called, consisted of some 70 structures containing well in excess of a million board feet of lumber. Single lumberjacks luxuriated in five huge two-story dormitories, two men to a room. Janitors cleaned the rooms and made the beds daily; the sheets were changed weekly. Married employees lived with their families in 46 individual cottages of three or four rooms each. The all-electric

Loggers at the Shaver Lake mill of the Fresno Flume and Lumber Company stand with their peaveys for the photographer about 1896. The peavey was a heavy-handled woods tool, with a spike point and a free-swinging hook, used in rolling logs. It was supposedly invented by one J.H. Peavey of Bangor, Maine.

dining hall seated 448 men at 56 eight-man tables, with a professional staff of cooks and waitresses providing restaurant-quality food and service.

A central system supplied water, electricity, steam heat, and sewage facilities to all buildings. Other amenities included a school, hospital, community hall, theater, post office, commissary, barber shop, pool hall, and tennis court. Until the distance to the cutting areas made it impractical in later years, workers were even transported on railroad cars back to Central Camp for a hot lunch at noon.

Sierra lumberjacks played as strenuously as they labored. The three "B's"—booze, brothels, and brawling—were the most popular forms of amusement, but fishing, hunting, gambling, and baseball games also drew their share of participants. On rare multi-day holidays such as the Fourth of July, riotous trips to the nearest San Joaquin Valley town were the preferred recreation. Here a man's hard-earned savings sometimes disappeared by noon the first day in town. At the conclusion of the holiday, the logging superintendent invariably had to bail out a goodly number of his employees who had run afoul of the local law.

Sierra lumber camps reflected the general prejudice of the times in America, with the various ethnic groups relegated to particular tasks depending on race or nationality. Almost all the higher-paying woods jobs were held by American-born workmen. More tedious work—bucking, swamping, and woodcutting—was largely performed by southern Europeans. Indians, Chinese, and Mexicans supplied the backbreaking labor required in railroad grading, chute building, and slash cleanup. Blacks, to put it simply, were never hired.

The modern Sierra logging scene bears little resemblance to times gone by. Nowadays, the typical lumberjack drives to work in the woods in his own pickup truck. He carries his chain saw, hard hat, and lunch bucket in the back. After a six- to eight-hour stint at good wages, with overtime pay for extra duty, he returns home to the family residence in a nearby town like most other working men. The job is still a hard and dangerous one, and steady employment is seldom guaranteed, but it's light years removed from the way it was in the days of steam.

Lumberjacks at Converse Basin were proud of their ability to log the big trees. Note the men standing on their companions' shoulders to emphasize the diameter of the log behind them. Several photographers in the Millwood area earned their livelihood for a time by taking pictures of the lumberjacks and then selling prints to the subjects. (Harold Schutt Collection)

Recreation

Booze and bawds were the favored pastimes of most Sierra lumberjacks. Loggers often spent their Sundays at the local whorehouse, if one was nearby. A happy customer relaxes with two of the girls **(facing page)** at the Madera Sugar Pine brothel known as "Tipperary," a semi-permanent house of prostitution near Fish Camp. The girls, who appear to be clean and not altogether unattractive, charged $2 a visit. Overnight stays cost $10.

Sunday boxing matches were also popular. Two Sanger Lumber Company loggers battle each other **(below)** in the Hume Lake ring about 1912.

Camp 1, on the northside logging show of the Yosemite Lumber Company **(right),** was a permanent installation. The big engine house and several comfortable residences provided above-average working and living conditions for camp employees.

The happy gentleman (below) is Ray ''Slim'' McGowan, foreman at the top of both Yosemite inclines for years. McGowan set the record for the fastest time down the first incline, using the sled described on page 66. The child does not seem nearly so pleased as Ray in this photograph. (Jim Law Collection)

The Sugar Pine Lumber Company's mountain facilities at Central Camp were perhaps the finest ever known in the industry. The five big dormitories are shown here, soon after construction in 1923.

The Madera Sugar Pine Company rebuilt its sawmill headquarters at Sugar Pine following the disastrous fire of September 9, 1922. Some of the new company houses, pictured in 1923, are still used as summer houses by current owners of the property.

Loggers line up for dinner in front of the cookhouse at the Shaver Lake mill of the Fresno Flume and Lumber Company in 1895 **(right).** This structure hardly compares to the commodious dining hall of the Sugar Pine Lumber Company at Central Camp **(below).** The main hall, 116 by 42 feet, seated 448 men at 56 eight-man tables. The decor was French ivory, with handsome light fixtures and a restful indirect lighting system. The 2,500-foot kitchen contained the most modern all-electric equipment available.

This rustic "church" was established at Converse Basin in 1903. Notice the hoist tracks in the foreground and the huge stack of firewood slabs in the rear.

A **better-than-average** portable house is shown **(below)** on the Sugar Pine Lumber Company's first-class Central camp operation.

The Portable Camp

Portable houses improved the lot of the Sierra lumberjack during the later years of railroad logging. A Forest Service report of 1917 describes the camp accommodations of the time as follows: ''To obviate the necessity of long walks to work, large logging camps must be moved at intervals of from one to three seasons. For this reason the portable camp is supplanting the old-style permanent type, which was torn down or abandoned at every move. The old type consisted of large bunkhouses, with double tiers of bunks down the sides. The initial cost of such camps is low, but they cannot be moved or kept free from vermin, and the men dislike them.

''The sleeping quarters in a portable camp are frame cabins, 10 by 18 feet. Low-grade lumber is used in their construction. The walls are battened and the roofs double-boarded or covered with tarpaper. Two skid timbers are placed lengthwise under each cabin to serve as a foundation and to facilitate moving. Each cabin accommodates four men in single bunks, or preferably on steel cots. There is also room for a stove and usually a small table. When it is desired to move to a new site, the cabins are loaded on flat cars by means of donkey engines. Ordinarily a camp can be moved in one day. Some operators place several cabins together end to end to form a portable cookhouse.

''Bedding is not furnished and mattresses but seldom, though each man is permitted to take enough hay for a bed. Small commissaries are provided in the larger camps, and sometimes a laundry and shower, for which each man is charged $2 a month.''

The Madera Sugar Pine Company's *Arthur Hill* **(right)** pushes a train of flat cars laden with portable houses to a new location along the logging railroad. (Craig Konklin Collection)

ARTHUR HILL
ARTHUR HILL

Sanger Lumber Company's Shay No. 2 was used as a stationary boiler by two different companies after the lumber operation was scrapped about 1928. The boiler is shown here at the Valley Paving Company plant in Fresno on November 10, 1941. The engine was totally scrapped by 1945. (Don DeVere Collection)

EPILOGUE

The Whistles Blow No More

THE STEAM-LOGGING ERA ENDED in the southern Sierra Nevada nearly half a century ago. Obvious traces of its existence are hard to find today even for the well-informed. If one is fortunate he might spot a rotting trestle or a pile of twisted wire rope somewhere along a back mountain road; maybe even the remnants of an old logging camp tucked deep in the forest; or perhaps a few broken bottles, a rusty railroad spike, or the indentation of a forgotten logging chute.

More obviously, there are the thriving communities that got their start as a result of the Sierra logging industry, which was once the second (next to agriculture) leading business in central California. The San Joaquin Valley towns of Pinedale, Madera, Sanger, Clovis, and Merced Falls owe their very life to the early lumber companies. In the Sierra Nevada, the resorts of Central Camp, Sugar Pine, Sequoia Lake, Hume Lake, and Shaver Lake came into being as logging camps. All through the mountains between Sequoia and Yosemite, hundreds of miles of old railroad grades provide convenient vehicular access to the back country. The main road from Fresno to Yosemite National Park, in fact, runs over a portion of the former Madera Sugar Pine right-of-way near Fish Camp (Highway 41).

As the years go by, and the memories of the few remaining oldtimers grow dim, fact has a way of fading into folklore. Somehow, as the stories are told and retold, the trees have a way of getting bigger, the flumes longer, the inclines steeper. This book was compiled in an effort to set the record straight while it's still possible—the facts really need no embellishment—and to preserve the pictorial story of an uncommon period in permanent form for the curious of the future.

★ ★ ★ ★

The steam-logging era was literally run by whistles. At the mountain mills, men went to work by whistle, began and finished lunch by whistle, and ended each shift at the whistle's command. Along the railroads, whistles sounded warnings or communicated information about train movements. In the woods, the whistle punk was an integral part of every yarding crew. Logging would have been virtually impossible without whistle signals from distant points.

The whistles blow no more in the mountains of the southern Sierra Nevada. They long ago succumbed to the diesel horn and the two-way radio. But the time and place they represented is surely worth remembering.

The upright posts of an old Fresno Flume and Lumber Company structure still stand near Shaver Lake. These appear to be the remains of a logging-chute trestle. (Bill Miles)

Betsy of Sugar Pine

Bill Fisher of Colfax, California, keeps the memory of *Betsy,* Madera Sugar Pine's No. 1 **(left),** alive on his Fisher Sugarpine Railroad. Fisher painstakingly built the live-steam model **(below)** from photographs of the original, despite having to guess at the exact dimensions because there were no records or plans to go by. Fisher's model has a boiler made of copper with bronze castings. The drivers are turned from ¾-inch plate steel, and the cylinders are made of Teflon. Except for three gears and a few fittings, Fisher fabricated all parts from scratch. The model burns manzanita wood and will climb a 4-percent grade. The riding car he uses behind the engine is a hollowed-out fir log, with space for extra water and wood, and a seat for the engineer-rider. Fisher runs his engine on 500 feet of track at his Colfax residence. (Bill Fisher)

The unusual harp switch stand shown here was found by a Fresno railfan along the former Pine Ridge Lumber Company right-of-way. (Bill Miles)

A Forest Service sign marks the approximate mill site of the old Pine Ridge operation, although both the spelling of the name "Peterson" and the dates in question are incorrect.

The abandoned grade of the Pine Ridge Lumber Company's three-mile railroad near Rush Creek is still plainly visible.

The Yosemite Mountain-Sugar Pine Railroad

Four miles south of Yosemite National Park, a steam-powered Shay still plies the slopes of the Sierra like some anachronistic reminder of days gone by. The Shay is the former West Side Lumber Company's No. 10, and it runs along a four-mile portion of the erstwhile right-of-way of the Madera Sugar Pine Company just below Fish Camp. The operation, known as the Yosemite Mountain-Sugar Pine Railroad, was built in the mid-1960s by Rudy Stauffer, a local resort owner, and his son Max. The railroad runs on a daily schedule during the summer months, and on a limited basis the rest of the year as weather permits.

Passengers are carried behind the locomotive on open flat cars, using cut-out logs as seats. The photographs **(above)** and **(facing page)** show the big three-truck, narrow-gauge Shay in action on the line. (Joe Bispo)

10

Yosemite Lumber Co.

The four photographs on these pages show remnants of the Yosemite Lumber Company's former logging operations near Yosemite National Park. A portable camp car **(above)** still stands at Camp 12 on the south side of the Merced River. The rustic shack **(left)** was once occupied by workers at the top of the first big incline. The remains of the only trestle on the south-side logging railroad **(opposite, top)** slowly succumb to the elements. The top of the second big incline at Trumbull Peak **(opposite, bottom)** is a conglomeration of crumbling concrete foundations, rotting timbers, and rusting pipes.

This beautiful shot by the renowned Sierra photographer Ansel Adams is perhaps the last picture ever taken of a Yosemite Valley Railroad train operating in

the Merced River Canyon. The scene shows YV No. 23 pulling flat cars loaded with ties, as the scrapper takes up the remains of the line in the fall of 1945.

This is the only long lumber flume still operating in the United States. Built by the Broughton Lumber Company of Underwood, Washington, in 1923, the flume runs nine miles down the Columbia Gorge from the sawmill at Willard to the planing mill at Underwood. The company ships up to 150,000 board feet of lumber each day, five days a week, and it takes less than an hour for a board to make the nine-mile journey. (Leon Callaway)

Index

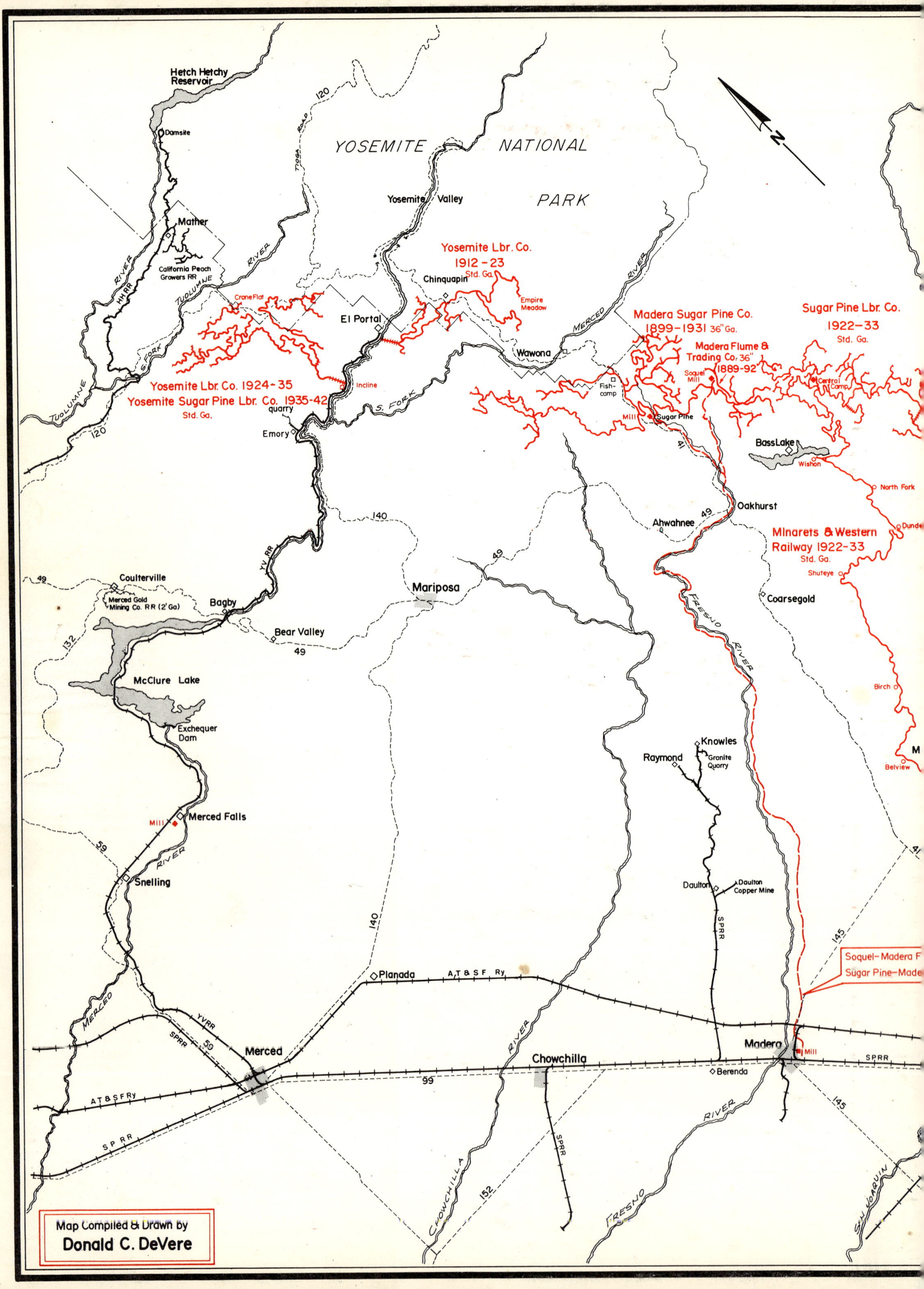

Hetch Hetchy Reservoir
Damsite
YOSEMITE NATIONAL PARK
TIOGA ROAD
120
Yosemite Valley
Mather
California Peach Growers RR
HH RR
TUOLUMNE RIVER
S. FORK
Yosemite Lbr. Co.
1912-23
Std. Ga.
Chinquapin
Empire Meadow
Crane Flat
El Portal
MERCED RIVER
Wawona
Madera Sugar Pine Co.
1899-1931 36" Ga.
Sugar Pine Lbr. Co.
1922-33
Std. Ga.
Madera Flume & Trading Co. 36"
1889-92
Soquel Mill
Central Camp
Fish-camp
Incline
Yosemite Lbr. Co. 1924-35
Yosemite Sugar Pine Lbr. Co. 1935-42
Std. Ga.
quarry
Emory
Mill
Sugar Pine
41
Bass Lake
Wishon
North Fork
Oakhurst
Ahwahnee
49
140
Dunde
Minarets & Western Railway 1922-33
Std. Ga.
Shuteye
YV RR
Coulterville
Merced Gold Mining Co. RR (2' Ga)
Bagby
Mariposa
Coarsegold
Bear Valley
132
FRESNO RIVER
McClure Lake
Exchequer Dam
Birch
Knowles
Raymond
Granite Quarry
Belview
Merced Falls
Mill
59
Snelling
Daulton
Daulton Copper Mine
SPRR
145
Soquel-Madera F
Sugar Pine-Made
Planada
A T & S F Ry
YVRR
Merced
Madera
Mill
Chowchilla
Berenda
99
CHOWCHILLA RIVER
152
FRESNO RIVER
SAN JOAQUIN
Map Compiled & Drawn by
Donald C. DeVere